MW01599294

PATTERNS OF INFLUENCE

PATTERNS

OF

INFLUENCE

Strategic Culture
Case Studies and Conclusions

Edited by Matthew R. Slater, PhD

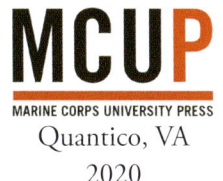

Quantico, VA
2020

LIBRARY OF CONGRESS CATALOGING-IN-PUBLICATION DATA

Names: Slater, Matthew R., editor.
Title: Patterns of influence : strategic culture case studies and conclusions / edited by Matthew R. Slater.
Description: First edition. | Quantico, VA : Marine Corps University Press, 2019. | Includes bibliographical references and index. | Summary: "This book addresses applied strategic culture and investigates the usefulness of the concept to better understand how internal state dynamics form unique institutions, behaviors, and perspectives that impact their external interactions with other states. The strategic culture literature successfully provides the necessary intellectual underpinnings; this volume is more concerned with its practical application for policy makers and analysts. This is accomplished by comparing a diverse set of case studies, including Afghanistan, Brazil, China, and Kosovo, to see if they use strategic culture consistently, which provides useful insights despite differences in state size and degree of political and social order"— Provided by publisher.
Identifiers: LCCN 2019028785 | ISBN 9781732003057 (paperback)
Subjects: LCSH: Strategic culture—Case studies. | International relations—Decision making—Case studies.
Classification: LCC U21.2 .P334 2019 | DDC 355/.0335—dc23
LC record available at https://lccn.loc.gov/2019028785

Marine Corps University Press
2044 Broadway Street
Quantico, VA 22134
www.usmcu.edu/mcupress

First edition published 2020
ISBN: 978-1-7320030-5-7

CONTENTS

FOREWORD

When the Cold War ended in 1991, we adjusted our national security strategy to address global instability. This took the American military to many places, such as Somalia and Iraq, where our forces engaged in persistent, low-intensity conflict. After the terrorist attacks on the United States on 11 September 2001, the American military deployed large numbers of forces to the greater Middle East—primarily in prolonged campaigns in Iraq and Afghanistan, but in other places too—to counter violent Islamic terrorism. As these campaigns wind down, once again the world is realigning, but this time into a multipolar power structure. *Patterns of Influence: Strategic Culture Case Studies and Conclusions* is a timely book because of its applicability to the emerging strategic environment. Not only can it help us understand emerging threats, but the strategic culture approach emphasized in this book can help us bridge the gap between academic and military disciplines.

Now that the United States finds itself once again in an era of great power competition, new and novel approaches will be needed to ensure peace and prosperity for our country, our allies, and partners. Strategic culture may not be a new approach—Jack L. Snyder wrote about it more than 50 years ago to help American strategists better anticipate the Soviet Union's counterstrategies to U.S. defense planning—but it has been underemphasized for several years. The emerging strategic environment is characterized by multipolarity, power balancing, selective engagement, and spheres of influence, among other trends. Understanding a country's strategic culture can aid U.S. policy makers in factoring in military capabilities, economic competition, and the unique proclivities of various countries in comprehensive U.S. military and diplomatic planning to advance American interests.

The strategic culture method emphasized in this book can be useful for professional military education. The military requires tangible outcomes for an investment of time and resources, just as any other practical endeavor. The strategic culture approach has the potential to enable military planners to inform us about the human aspects as well as the unique cultures found in different operational environments. A thorough understanding of history and culture lets us know about the cultural fault lines of a given country, which can help the American military navigate difficult human terrain. Strategic culture is particularly important for information operations because we must be able to understand the adversary well enough to shape their courses of action *before* conflict erupts, or we risk being shaped by their counterintelligence and information offensive efforts.

Patterns of Influence performs an important function by informing readers about the strategic cultures of China, Afghanistan, Brazil, and Kosovo. *Patterns of Influence* also advises practitioners on the pitfalls and best practices when applying the strategic culture method.

Brigadier General William J. Bowers
President and Commanding General
Marine Corps University
July 2017–July 2019

ACKNOWLEDGMENTS

I want to thank George Dallas for his unwavering support for the book. The MCU Press team was exceptional throughout the publication process, particularly Angela Anderson and Jason Gosnell for assisting with title selection, book cover design, and timely editing. Alexandra Kindell played an important role by providing editorial assistance and helping to launch the project.

PATTERNS OF INFLUENCE

INTRODUCTION

by Matthew R. Slater, PhD

Approach and Overview

This book addresses applied strategic culture and investigates the usefulness of the concept to better understand how internal state dynamics form unique institutions, behaviors, and perspectives that impact their external interactions with other states. The strategic culture literature successfully provides the necessary intellectual underpinnings; this volume is more concerned with its practical application for policy makers and analysts. The authors accomplish this by comparing a diverse set of case studies, including Afghanistan, Brazil, China, and Kosovo, to see if the strategic culture approach provides a deeper understanding about their policies and decision-making outcomes despite differences in state size and degree of political and social order.

Strategic culture is an intuitive concept that has endured over the years since it was introduced to the academic lexicon by Jack L. Snyder.[1] Both *strategy* and *culture* are broad academic terms that develop a more specific meaning when brought together. Colin S. Gray writes that strategy "should be thought

---

[1] Snyder states: "It is useful to look at the Soviet approach to strategic thinking as a unique 'strategic culture.' Individuals are socialized into a distinctively Soviet mode of strategic thinking. As a result of this socialization process, a set of general beliefs, attitudes, and behavioral patterns with regard to nuclear strategy has achieved a state of semipermanence that places them on the level of 'culture' rather than mere 'policy'." Jack L. Snyder, *The Soviet Strategic Culture: Implications for Limited Nuclear Operations* (Santa Monica, CA: Rand, 1977), v.

3

of as glue that holds together the purposeful activities of a state."[2] He explains that "strategy can be considered a system that enables functional cooperation among categorically distinctive behaviours in the interest of advancing some common purpose."[3] Strategy may be thought of as the glue, but culture informs us about the environment or conditions that impact the glue's resiliency or strength. Each state makes distinct decisions about its *strategy* under circumstances unique from other states and *culture* refers to these distinctive qualities.

The study of strategic culture consists of both the logical and seemingly illogical elements of state decision making. Strategic culture research helps us to understand the unique elements of a given state (e.g., historical narrative, political structure, or social organization) and informs us of how states interact with other actors. The strategic culture lens can, at minimum, provide the researcher with a contextual framework for understanding state decisions—and perhaps in some cases allow the researcher to predict a state's range of reactions to situations.

The case studies presented in this book highlight important and diverse questions regarding the practical application of the strategic culture concept. For example, is strategic culture more appropriate for states with reconciled identities, such as Brazil and China, rather than newly formed states still adapting to social and political transformation, such as Kosovo and Afghanistan? Politically coherent states possess clearly defined organizations and processes and newer states typically lack the traditions, organizational maturity, and cohesiveness to generate repeating patterns of behavior. If strategic culture is only useful to assess "stable" states, then its utility for analysts and

---

[2] Colin S. Gray, *The Future of Strategy* (Cambridge, UK: Polity Press, 2015), 23.
[3] Gray, *The Future of Strategy*, 23.

academics is somewhat restricted. However, strategic culture may be of use by shedding light on previously unthought of or nascent institutions that are generating some level of consistent state behavior and leading toward formative strategic culture.

The case studies in this volume address the usefulness of strategic culture regarding small states. Because smaller states are always heavily influenced by the actions of their larger or more powerful neighbors, is it advantageous to study their internal history, structures, and processes? Should a researcher spend a greater portion of their time examining more powerful regional states that may be the true source of small state strategic culture? The comparison of diverse case studies may provide insights to this complex question.

The second section of this introduction provides a brief summary of the development of strategic culture, orienting the reader to the strategic culture approach. The primary tenet of strategic culture is the notion that the strategy-making process and resulting policies are the output of both culture and power considerations. This seems intuitive, but until Snyder gave prominence to the field of study, the role of culture in state behavior was frequently overlooked in favor of a given state's economic power and military capability. Other writers, most notably Gray and Alastair Iain Johnston, continue to debate and enrich the field of study.

The third section makes the argument that strategic culture may be useful to international studies, but it also defies conventional theoretical approaches because it encourages the researcher to consider multiple levels of analysis simultaneously. J. David Singer warned us that researching more than one level of analysis at a time could be problematic because they are inherently distinct.[4] Robert D. Putnam presents a two-level approach that combines the domestic and international levels and offers a method to bridge the theoretical gap. Peter Alexis Gourevitch takes the argument full circle and contends that the domestic and international levels are intertwined and should always be considered together in any comprehensive assessment.

This introduction provides a preview of the five chapters that comprise this book, which begins with a strategic culture framework proposal and is followed by four case studies. The last section of the introduction also proposes questions for the reader to consider while reading through the case studies. These questions are addressed in the conclusion of the book.

The Development of the Strategic Culture Approach

The strategic culture body of literature has matured during the last 40 years, from its introduction as a new concept that generated debate regarding its theoretical value, to more recent discussions regarding its utility to international relations practitioners. The term *strategic culture* was first coined by Snyder in a research report titled *The Soviet Strategic Culture: Implications for Limited Nuclear Operations.* The term gained recognition and today it is a widely accepted approach in international relations.[5] The ideas in Snyder's work challenged conventional thinking at the time that tended to rely on rational actor as-

---

[4] J. David Singer, "The Level-of-Analysis Problem in International Relations," *World Politics* 14, no. 1 (October 1961): 78, https://doi.org/10.2307/2009557. Singer states that "we have, in our texts and elsewhere, roamed up and down the ladder of organizational complexity with remarkable abandon, focusing upon the total system, international organizations, regions, coalitions, extra-national associations, nations, domestic pressure groups, social classes, elites and individuals as the needs of the moment required." He notes that researchers' propensity for "vertical drift" causes methodological instability.

[5] Please see chapter 1 for a more thorough overview of the development and definition of *strategic culture.*

sumptions and discounted cultural influences. He questioned the notion that Soviet military planners and policy makers would follow the same logic as their U.S. counterparts on the limited use of nuclear weapons:

Will the Soviets agree to play according to the ill-understood and esoteric rules of intrawar deterrence—a notion that Soviet writings characterize as "abstract from life"? Or will they see any limited nuclear attack as voiding all rules of restraint, presaging inevitable escalation?[6]

Snyder warned U.S. strategists about the dangers of ethnocentrism and determined that the contrast in Soviet and American approaches stemmed from a true difference in perspectives based on preexisting cultural beliefs rather than an intent to manipulate and deceive.[7]

After the end of the Cold War, other authors built on Snyder's work. Gray wrote that public, strategic, and military-organizational aspects of strategic culture are all important, but he warned about the concept's inherit limitations: "The needs of theory building and the reality of culture's ubiquitous contextuality, are, alas, severely at odds."[8] He understood strategic culture as an organic element to any assessment of state behavior, but due to the pervasive nature of culture it is "deadly for the practicality, let alone the utility of theory."[9] Although Gray acknowledges the importance of strategic culture, he warned against using it as the sole means to examine state relations: "Culture matters deeply. . . . But, it is not all that matters in strategy and security."[10]

---

[6] Snyder, *The Soviet Strategic Culture*, 2.
[7] Snyder, *The Soviet Strategic Culture*, 38.
[8] Colin S. Gray, *Out of the Wilderness: Prime Time for Strategic Culture* (Fort Belvoir, VA: Defense Threat Reduction Agency Advanced Systems and Concepts Office, 2006), 26.
[9] Gray, *Out of the Wilderness*, 26.
[10] Gray, *Out of the Wilderness*, 4.

Johnston is another important voice in the strategic culture dialogue. Johnston finds common ground with Gray, but he also diverges on the question of theoretical potential. Johnston agrees with Gray's interpretation that "the concept of strategic culture is viewed as an amalgam of a wide range of (potentially competing) variables or inputs."[11] Unlike Gray, Johnston states that it is imperative to apply a structure to strategic culture inquiry to make the concept theoretically rigorous. During his survey of the literature, Johnston noted that there are broad differences of opinion regarding the assumption that strategic culture plays any role in state behavior, or whether it is the sole determining factor.[12] Johnston warned that strategic culture should be applied with a great deal of caution because findings suggest an irregular pattern of influence in state behavior that would greatly diminish strategic culture's explanatory potential.

Considering Domestic Sources of State Behavior

Despite the theoretical problems surrounding the use of strategic culture, international relations scholars have long recognized the need to account for the domestic sources of state behavior. The value of strategic culture is based on the depth of understanding it provides about the statements, policies, and actions of leaders and institutions. For example, some may find China's aggressive posture in the South China Sea inexplicable due to the billions of dollars in trade that supports friendly economic ties throughout the Pacific, or Brazil's prevailing belief that state, nonstate actors, and foreign powers may use environmental concerns as a reason to invade and occupy the Amazon.[13] Looking at circumstances through the lens of political

---

[11] Alastair Iain Johnston, "Thinking about Strategic Culture," *International Security* 19, no. 4 (Spring 1995): 33n2, https://doi.org/10.2307/2539119.
[12] Johnston, "Thinking about Strategic Culture," 63.
[13] These issues are addressed in chapter 2 on China and in chapter 3 on Brazil.

and economic rationality, one could assume China would take a multilateral approach to security interests in the South China Sea. In the case of Brazil, it is highly unlikely any state would take the risks necessary to invade and occupy the Amazon, even though the environment is a growing concern with the international community. Strategic culture helps explain the gap existing between the seemingly irrational and unpredictable behavior of states (as viewed by outsiders) by addressing the roots of domestic influences on state strategies and policies. Strategic culture holds the promise to illuminate *why* a state behaves in a certain way, and it also sheds light on *how* their internal narrative shapes the conditions of policy making.

The ambition of explaining the role of internal influences on state behavior is not unique to strategic culture. Research executed by Singer, Putnam, and Gourevitch attempted to bridge this gap, with each author using a distinctive approach. Singer's research emphasized a rigorous *levels of analysis* methodology that acknowledges the legitimacy of both domestic and international factors but within their unique contexts. His utilitarian model insists that a debate concerning the primacy of one level over the other must be preceded by an acknowledgment of what the researcher is trying to study. An impartial researcher should be able to reduce distortions on their topic, or focus on the level where "distortion is least dysfunctional and where such accuracy is absolutely essential."[14] In other words, optimization at a chosen level of analysis will suboptimize research at the other levels.[15] In his final analysis, Singer reviews the advantages and disadvantages of each level: the in-

---

[14] Singer, "The Level-of-Analysis Problem in International Relations," 79.

[15] Singer delineates two levels of analysis in his 1961 article, including the international system and the state. International relations literature addresses many other levels, such as the individual, global, regional, and subnational identity. In *Patterns of Influence,* the authors address most of their work at the state or domestic level, however, Tashev leaves the door open to other possibilities that he addresses in his framework discussion in chapter 1.

ternational relations level provides a more comprehensive and coherent view, whereas the domestic view provides richer detail and depth.

Putnam, like Singer, takes an ambivalent view regarding the importance of the international system compared to domestic variables, however, unlike Singer he tries to bring the two levels together to explain state behavior.[16] He emphasizes how decision makers must simultaneously take international and domestic considerations into account; therefore, it is impossible to declare the primacy of one level over another or ignore the importance of one at the expense of the other. Putnam discusses the dynamic linkages not only between levels but also how one dyad affects the same linkages in different issue areas. For instance, an agreement reached about a border dispute may demonstrate the effects of international pressure on a state, but the resulting internal schisms may weaken a leader and cause the state to back away from future agreements. This dyad may affect other issues such as security. If a leader was viewed as too conciliatory about a trade issue, it might explain why they became hawkish in other areas of foreign policy. Putnam states, "It is fruitless to debate whether domestic politics really determine international relations, or the reverse. The answer to that question is clearly 'Both, sometimes'."[17]

Using state-level policy decisions to explain international conflict, or the possibility of conflict, is not unusual in international studies, particularly in the field of political economy. Gourevitch offers an observation on the European interwar years: "International cooperation on policy survives so long as the political forces committed to its continuation within each

---

[16] Robert D. Putnam, "Diplomacy and Domestic Politics: The Logic of Two-Level Games," *International Organization* 42, no. 3 (Summer 1988): 460.

[17] Putnam, "Diplomacy and Domestic Politics," 427.

country are able to prevail."[18] He explains how the international economy of the period was a product of the national processes and policies where "political institutions, politicians, leaders and interest groups interact."[19] The domestic choices of each state converged with those of other states to produce global results; the choices of domestic actors matter more than external variables, such as the international structure. Although Gourevitch did not focus on the topic of security, he offered a clear explanation of how the internal dynamics of states affect state and international behavior.

Each author contributes an important theoretical perspective to the holistic approach of strategic culture. Singer tells us that there is no competition between the levels of analysis—only distinction. Therefore, unlike structural philosophy, the utility of a given level of analysis is determined by the issue under consideration. Putnam provides us with a logical narrative that allows us to sidestep Singer's warnings about moving between levels because he recognizes the need to bring domestic and international levels of analysis into the conversation simultaneously. Gourevitch provides us with examples when the domestic level must be explored as the root cause of outcomes at the international level, even in cases when the international level may play an important role in outcomes. Strategic culture takes a primarily domestic-level view, but counter to traditional schools of thought, cuts across the levels of analysis to exam-

---

[18] Peter Alexis Gourevitch, "Squaring the Circle: The Domestic Sources of International Cooperation," *International Organization* 50, no. 2 (Spring 1996): 354, https://doi.org/10.1017/S0020818300028599. While reviewing Barry Eichengreen's *Golden Fetters: The Gold Standard and the Great Depression, 1919–1939* (New York: Oxford University Press, 1995) and Beth A. Simmons's *Who Adjusts?: Domestic Sources of Foreign Economic Policy during the Interwar Years* (Princeton, NJ: Princeton University Press, 1994), Gourevitch gives examples of domestic sources of economic policies, such as Germany's reparations, wartime debts, shifts in production, and the structural effects of new technologies.

[19] Gourevitch, "Squaring the Circle," 352.

ine the role of leadership (individual level), regional actors and international organizations (international level), and internal bureaucracies and subgroups (state level) simultaneously.

Organization

This book embraces the theoretical ambiguity of strategic culture, consciously recognizing the trade-off of increased flexibility and the sacrifice of theoretical rigor. In the first chapter, Blagovest Tashev proposes a well-researched framework that provides practitioners with potential sources of strategic culture. Tashev includes some variables that are not typical for strategic culture studies but purposefully casts a wide net to provide an inclusive method for researchers. His overview of strategic culture literature provides the reader with a reference for the diverse case studies presented in this volume. After an examination of strategic culture primary literature, he introduces the components of his framework with their associated explanations and examples. These components draw from both culturalist and realist approaches, as well as the domestic and international levels of analysis that provide a high level of flexibility for the practitioner.[20]

Most strategic culture case studies presented in the next chapters deal with the dilemma of identifying coherent security policy or strategic-level trends: such is not the problem with the case study on China. Christopher D. Yung provides

---

[20] John Glenn's summary of the classic neorealist (or structuralist) argument illustrates how it differs from strategic culturalists. Neorealists assume a range of predictable behavior by states, known as the rational actor assumption. They hold that because state behavior is heavily influenced by the presence of anarchy, their choices are narrow; there is little to be learned from studying the unique aspects of a state. Culturalists think the opposite: state actions shape the international system and should be assessed by their own unique characteristics. See John Glenn, "Realism versus Strategic Culture: Competition and Collaboration?," *International Studies Review* 11, no. 3 (2009): 523–51, https://doi.org/10.1111/j.1468-2486 .2009.00872.x.

the reader with a succinct overview of 4,000 years of Chinese strategic culture to determine if current strategic behavior is influenced by identifiable sources. He points out that it is possible for researchers to explain any potential strategic culture outcome based on any specific era of China's long and diverse history. Therefore, his challenge is to identify key characteristics of current strategic behavior and determine its origins from the vast backdrop of Chinese history.

Vern Liebl provides a revealing case study about the strategic culture of Afghanistan that asks a key question: Does Afghanistan have a strategic culture? Liebl explains the nuanced political and ethnic situation in Afghanistan, concluding that Afghanistan should be regarded as a single political entity. He refers to the 14 ethnic groups mentioned in the Afghan national anthem as an example of its disaggregated nature. Liebl's chapter questions the usefulness of the strategic culture perspective to developing countries that lack the fundamental coherence to be considered a legitimate state. He calls Afghanistan a "nation of nations." Can one realistically expect to find a collective narrative associated with strategic culture in a politically and ethnically fractured state? Through historical analysis, Liebl shows us how there can be identity within disunity that helps us to test the practical limits of strategic culture application.

Denise Slater provides a well-researched chapter concerning the strategic culture of Brazil. Unlike many developing countries in the region, the Brazilian national narrative has now become unified after a series of historical events shaping their collective perceptions and fears. Denise Slater addresses the country's strategic culture by identifying its primary tenets. She uses the assumption of a state's emotionality, or seemingly irrational decisions, beliefs, or narrative to analyze that country's strategic culture. Her analysis presents additional insights to understand Brazilian policies and actions regarding the Amazon. It also contradicts the notion of states as rational actors, or at least expands the boundaries on the composition of rational actor behavior. By citing mostly Brazilian sources and strategy documents, she shows how policy makers, both military and civilian, are seemingly convinced of the possibility of a foreign occupation of the Amazon. What unique strategic culture narratives are consistently pushing Brazilian leaders in this direction, and why do they exist? Slater provides a definitive assessment and application of strategic culture elements and concepts in such a way that it enriches the body of literature on the subject and demonstrates the value of the strategic culture perspective.

George Bogden writes a richly detailed chapter on Kosovo that challenges the traditional notions of national identity. Like Afghanistan, Kosovo possesses a fractured national identity. In Kosovo's case, the discontinuity is related to the high degree of control exerted by the European Union and the internal debates regarding regional and internal security. Unlike Afghanistan, Kosovo is a relatively new state. Strategic culture literature assumes a historical coherence and continuity that cannot be claimed by new states. Does this mean the application of strategic culture in these cases is a fruitless endeavor? Bogden will provide an interesting answer to this question, which may provide ideas to other researchers about the challenges associated with nascent strategic cultures.

CHAPTER
1

A STRATEGIC CULTURE FRAMEWORK FOR PRACTITIONERS

by Blagovest Tashev, PhD

Introduction

This chapter links the concept of culture to the understanding of a state's decision making and behavior in international relations. For this purpose, it introduces the concept of strategic culture and its evolution, demonstrating how the concept of strategic culture can be used to understand national decision making and discern the range of probable actions a state is likely to take internationally to pursue its interests.

The dominant approach to the study of international relations and foreign policy, often called *realism*, studies the material characteristics of the environment to understand the behavior of the state. This approach views the international environment through the lens of the distribution of military, economic, and favorable demographics among states, also called the *balance of power*. The greater the capabilities of a state compared to the capabilities of another, the greater the power of the first state. This distribution of material capabilities determines the outcome in interactions between states. What states do and how they do it is determined by the relative power they have.

Larger states, possessing greater economies, more powerful militaries, and larger populations are expected to achieve their goals when confronting smaller states, which accordingly possess less capability. Similarly, an alliance of states that possesses greater capabilities than another alliance is expected to dominate a conflict (any conflict, not just violent ones) between the two. Even when the relationships between states are not violent, the nature of the states' preferences, goals, and behaviors are supposed to be determined by the relative material power of each state.

Proponents of this logic developed the *rational actor model* to analyze state behavior. This model assumes that decision makers are rational in the sense that they would choose actions that help them achieve their goals.[1] The rational actor model sees the foreign policy choices states make in pursuit of survival and security as products of the following sequence: When confronted by a problem, the rational decision maker identifies the foreign-policy goals and prioritizes them. Then the various available options in pursuit of these goals are analyzed and ranked according to the likelihood of success and the costs and benefits associated with each option. The decision maker then chooses the highest-ranked choice among the options.

This model has been constantly modified in an attempt to improve its analytical power and in response to numerous criticisms pointing out various shortcomings. For example, many point out that the model assumes decision makers have all the information they need to make the best decision, an

---

[1] For an overview of realism's assumptions, including the rational actor assumption, see Robert Keohane, ed., *Neorealism and Its Critics* (New York: Columbia University Press, 1986); and Miles Kahler, "Rationality in International Relations," *International Organization* 52, no. 4 (Autumn 1998): https://doi.org/10.1162/002081898550680.

assumption easily undermined by lessons from real-life crises.[2] Others point out that the model does not take into consideration that once the final decision has been made, it might not be ideally implemented, as it is various agencies with their own often divergent preferences and goals that are entrusted with the execution of the decision.

Realism is challenged by the idea that states are embedded in state and international environments that have not only a material but also a cultural dimension.[3] Cultural factors influence the state and its elites in a variety of ways. Cultural factors affect the way the world is perceived by state elites and society; impact the definition of enduring national interests; influence the goals the state seeks to obtain; predispose the state elite and society toward certain actions and policies rather than others; limit the number of options that are considered possible and available; influence the way options are assessed; and affect how policies are enacted. Accordingly, *culturalist* approaches to the study of states' approaches to security focus on a range of topics, including the effects of domestic political cultures, the ways the cultures of various state institutions responsible for ensuring national security affect their functions, the effect of domestic attitudes and assumptions about the use of force on the way the state uses force, and the influence of culture on crafting and executing security and defense strategies. The culturalists' argument is that a state's behavior is influenced not only by their physical capabilities and how they relate to the capabilities of other states but also by domestic, nonmaterial factors.

In addition to the internal environment, the external cul-

---

[2] After the end of the Cold War, for example, American historians were finally able to research Soviet archives and consequently gain a more realistic understanding of Moscow's past goals, motivations, and views. See John Lewis Gaddis, *We Now Know: Rethinking Cold War History* (New York: Oxford University Press, 1997).

[3] For a review of the culturalist approaches to international relations, see Michael C. Desch, "Culture versus Structure in Post-9/11 Security Studies," *Strategic Insights* 4, no. 10 (October 2005).

tural environment, too, has a powerful influence on states' behavior. There are at least three layers to the international environment in which the states operate that influence strategic culture.[4] First, there are international institutions, ranging from the formal organizations—the United Nations (UN), the North Atlantic Treaty Organization (NATO), European Union (EU), Organization of American States (OAS), Association of Southeast Asian Nations (ASEAN), among many others—to treaties and regimes—the Treaty on the Non-Proliferation of Nuclear Weapons, Strategic Arms Reduction Treaty, and the like. Another layer is a world political culture. It includes elements like rules of sovereignty and international law as well as transnational political discourse carried out by international movements and players like Doctors without Borders and the Catholic Church. The third layer includes patterns of amity and enmity based on culture, ideologies, and practices. For example, studies point out that, although all states may participate in violent conflict with other states, democracies do not fight other democracies. Although studies have advanced several explanations for this pattern, they agree that democracies share some cultural and institutional characteristics that prevent them from fighting each other.

Importantly, cultural environments, both state and international, affect not only the incentives for various kinds of decisions made by the state but also the state's identity. This refers to the basic character of the state, its collective self-image, and its perception of its proper role and behavior in the international system. Studies investigate influences from history, geography, ideas, texts, and experiences that have an impact on the

---

[4] The discussion in this chapter on the international cultural environment adopts concepts and ideas from Peter J. Katzenstein, ed., *The Culture of National Security: Norms and Identities in World Politics* (New York: Columbia University Press, 1996), 34.

state's strategic identity over time. Researchers are particularly interested in the state's formative early years as they are thought to have a significant and long-lasting impact on its identity in general and strategic culture in particular.

This author subscribes to the notion that the successful study of state behavior requires an approach that integrates material and cultural elements.[5] It is important to note that most culturalists do not deny the importance of material causes, such as the relative military, economic, and demographic capabilities, but they point out that attempts to explain the behavior of states solely in terms of material factors are unconvincing.[6] In other words, culturalist approaches to the study of international relations and foreign policy should be seen as an attempt to supplement dominant realist theories rather than supplant them.

This chapter proceeds with an introduction to the concept of strategic culture, including its evolution. It then adopts a working definition of strategic culture and a model for its analysis. The model includes variables, the most important cultural tenets that affect a state's security policy and behavior. The chapter then introduces the most important tenets of the international cultural environment that also shape the state's policy and behavior. The concluding section of this chapter in-

[5] Others, however, argue that realism and strategic culture are at the opposite ends of the spectrum, because they adopt different levels of analysis—strategic culture focuses on the state and society, while the realists direct attention to the structure of the international system in their search for explanations for state behavior. Currently, the authors applying the strategic culture approach broadly agree that culture influences strategy in addition to any external material forces. States confront distinctive geostrategic problems through the prism of their individual strategic culture while having unique sets of capabilities and liabilities. For further discussion, see John Glenn et al., eds., *Neorealism versus Strategic Culture* (Burlington, VT: Ashgate Publishing Limited, 2004).

[6] Although realists do not dismiss culture as a factor, they consider it as merely an intervening variable that may influence behavior, largely having a secondary importance to material variables.

cludes research questions aiding the analysis of the domestic and international variables shaping the state's strategic culture.

Strategic Culture: Past to Present

The beginning of the modern exploration into the role of culture in state behavior can be traced back to 1977 when Jack L. Snyder proposed that American and Soviet nuclear strategies were products of different organizational, historical, and political contexts.[7] Snyder developed his argument to address defense planners' inability to anticipate the responses of Soviet nuclear strategists to American moves. Heavily influenced by the rational actor model and game theories, American nuclear planners expected their Soviet counterparts to have similar attitudes, assumptions, and beliefs about nuclear weapons and their use. Instead, Snyder suggested that the strategic elites of the two countries had separate cultures related to military and strategic affairs, including distinct beliefs, attitudes, assumptions, and behavioral patterns regarding nuclear strategy. He posited that these cultures do not exist in a vacuum, but instead they were manifestations of a society's culture in relation to security and the use of force, acquired through a socialization process. Notably, Snyder argues that because of this socialization process, the set of beliefs, attitudes, and behavior patterns achieves a level of culture, rather than a level of mere policy. In other words, the set of beliefs is semipermanent and not easily changed.

Snyder argued that strategic culture has an independent influence on strategic policy patterns. He speculates that Russia's long history of insecurity and authoritarian rule conditions the military's preference for offensive, preemptive military actions when confronting a threat. Despite his novel focus on cultural factors, however, Snyder did not explore the role of Communist ideology on Soviet strategic thinking. This is rath-

---

[7] Snyder, *The Soviet Strategic Culture.*

er remarkable given the ideology's extensive focus of the nature of conflict and war in the modern era, including clearly defined and constantly reinforced axioms among all strata of society.

Snyder was not alone in the exploration of cultural influences in strategic policies, especially in the context of the Cold War confrontation between the United States and the Soviet Union. Ken Booth and Colin S. Gray investigated the link between strategic culture and the superpowers' strategies related to weapons of mass destruction.[8] In this early period, the proponents of the strategic culture approach focused mostly on the two superpowers and did not develop a robust theoretical foundation for the study of state behavior that accommodates cultural factors. Most important, the dominant school in international relations—realism—dismissed the value of culture as an independent variable that helped to explain a state's security behavior. The end of the Cold War decreased scholars' interest in exploring what drives the nuclear strategies of superpowers; similarly, interest in strategic culture diminished.

The concept of strategic culture attracted attention once again in the 1990s and the 2000s. The study of strategic culture broke away from its initial focus on nuclear strategy and researchers began to examine other security issues.[9] What partially accounts for the renewed interests were the failure of realism to anticipate the end of the Cold War and the growing

---

[8] Ken Booth, *Strategy and Ethnocentrism* (New York: Routledge, 1979); Colin S. Gray, "National Style in Strategy: The American Example," *International Security* 6, no. 2 (Fall 1981); Colin S. Gray, "Comparative Strategic Culture," *Parameters* 14, no. 4 (Winter 1984); and Colin S. Gray, *Nuclear Strategy and National Style* (Lanham, MD: Hamilton Press, 1986).

[9] This came as no surprise as authors investigated the strategic cultures of nonnuclear states. Authors also began to focus on strategic behavior that was not explicitly related to the use of force. For example, official documents on the strategic culture of the European Union explicitly explored the nonmilitary, soft power strategy of the European Union. See *European Security Strategy: A Secure Europe in a Better World* (Brussels, Belgium: European Union External Action Service, 2003); and see also a special issue of *Oxford Journal on Good Governance* 2, no. 1 (March 2005).

influence of constructivism in international-relations theory. In fact, some authors believe culturalist approaches can be a better predictor of state behavior and outcomes in international relations than what they consider to be a discredited realist approach.[10] Constructivism, for its part, provided insights into the influences of domestic society and politics on a state's identity and actions in international relations. Scholars applied culture to explain how states crafted and reproduced strategic policies to create and maintain particular power relationships at home and abroad. The renewed interest in strategic culture was also accompanied by a more rigorous examination of theoretical and methodological issues. Many students of the subject were critical of the existing models because they struggled to separate independent from dependent variables.

Explorations in strategic culture also exposed the lack of a common approach to the study of the subject matter and deep disagreements about issues of definitions and methodologies. The most prominent of those disagreements was the debate between Colin S. Gray and Alastair Iain Johnston. Johnston sought to bring more methodological rigor to the study by avoiding the vague definition of culture and by distinguishing between culture and behavior. *Culture*, in his view, was "an integrated system of symbols (i.e., argumentation structures, languages, analogies, metaphors, etc.) that acts to establish pervasive and long-lasting grand strategic preferences."[11] Johnston treated culture as an independent variable that affects the dependent variable, strategic behavior.[12] In his study of Chinese strategic culture, Johnston investigates the effect of culture on

---

[10] Glenn et al., *Neorealism versus Strategic Culture*; and John S. Duffield et al., "Ism and Schisms: Culturalism versus Realism in Security Studies," *International Security* 24, no. 1 (Summer 1999): 156–80, https://doi.org/10.1162/016228899560086.

[11] Alastair Iain Johnston, *Cultural Realism: Strategic Culture and Grand Strategy in Chinese History* (Princeton, NJ: Princeton University Press, 1995), 36.

[12] Johnston, "Thinking about Strategic Culture," 36.

military strategy.[13] Gray, however, considered it a mistake to distinguish culture from behavior. Instead, he argued that strategic culture "should be approached both as a shaping context for behavior and itself as a constituent of that behavior."[14]

Researchers and writers were also split on the explanatory power of strategic culture. Some of them who were very critical of the realist approach asserted that strategic culture, rather than the material distribution of power, provided a better explanation of state behavior. Others, while critical of realism, did not discount material factors and instead argued that strategic culture complements the dominant school of thought.

In addition to exploring the content of the concept, they also deliberated on the sources of strategic culture. Once again, no consensus emerged. However, in a review of the literature, Darryl Howlett noted that the "most frequently cited sources of strategic culture are: geography, climate and resources; history and experience; political structure; the nature of organizations involved in defense; myths and symbols; key texts that inform actors of appropriate strategic action; and transnational norms, generational change and the role of technology."[15]

The concept of strategic culture deals with the relationship between culture and strategy. Culture concerns how people and groups view the world, make sense of what they observe, make decisions, and act. Culture includes several key factors: it is shared among people of a particular group; it provides the foundation of a worldview; and it helps us interpret the actions of individuals and events in the world. One problematic quality for researchers is that all aspects of culture are interrelated,

---

[13] Johnston, *Cultural Realism*.

[14] Colin S. Gray, "Strategic Culture as Context: The First Generation of Theory Strikes Back," *Review of International Studies* 25, no. 1 (January 1999): 50, https://doi.org/10.1017/S0260210599000492.

[15] Darryl Howlett, "Strategic Culture: Reviewing Recent Literature," *Strategic Insights* 6, no. 10 (November 2005).

making it fluid and dynamic. This makes it difficult to identify with a high degree of certainty cultural patterns and their relative impact.

We should not use culture as the only way to explain the behavior of states in international relations. There is always a danger to misuse culture in the analysis of state behavior. It is misleading to present culture as something out there—independent of people—an unchanging set of rules, beliefs, and norms that control human action. Instead, culture must be thought of as patterns of meaning and behavior created, maintained, and changed by people. These patterns emerge, endure, and change by people repeating them. People live culturally rather than live in culture. It is also important to point out that these patterns are not perfectly shared by all members of the group, which explains variations in behavior.

The term *strategy* refers to the way military power is used by states in the pursuit of national interests. Some researchers conceive of strategy to include not only military options as a means of attaining objectives but also economic and diplomatic pursuits. In this context, the concept is conceived as the coordinated use of all elements of national power to attain security-related national goals in response to external threats and risks.[16]

Regardless of which definition of strategy one adopts, a strategic culture approach investigates the relevance of cultural contexts in influencing strategy, including strategic preferences and choices. If strategy refers to the way a state uses the instruments at its disposal (or only military power) in the pursuit of the state's interest, the strategic culture approach helps us understand how the cultural context shapes interests, preferences, and choices as well as how the state goes about pursuing them.

When we refer to American strategic culture, for example,

---

[16] For more on strategy, see Gray, *The Future of Strategy*; and Williamson Murray et al., eds., *The Making of Strategy: Rulers, States, and War* (Cambridge, UK: Cambridge University Press, 1994).

we suggest that the United States has a distinct way of looking at and understanding the world and its place in it—and of acting strategically based on this. This also means that China has a distinct way of seeing the world and itself. China therefore acts and responds differently in pursuit of its national interests.

The idea of incorporating culture into the study of state security behavior is not new. Thucydides's *The History of the Peloponnesian War*, for example, attributes differences in the behavior of the warring parties to cultural differences among the city-states.[17] Thucydides does not explain the causes and conduct of hostilities between the city-states by the distribution of power among them but by the differences in national character and the character of the leadership. Similarly, Gray points out that, according to Carl von Clausewitz, the object of war is "to impose our will on the enemy," and thus the strength of the enemy's will is the subject of cultural inquiry.[18]

A Definition and Methodology

Although the study of strategic cultures became a prominent approach in the study of national security, there is no widely accepted definition of what precisely strategic culture is. Jack Snyder, a pioneer in the field, sees strategic culture as a "set of semi-permanent elite beliefs, attitudes, and behavior patterns socialized into a distinctive mode of thought."[19] Booth, in one of the more popular attempts in the formative years of the field, defined it as

> *a nation's traditions, values, attitudes, patterns of behavior, habits, symbols, achievements and particular ways of*

---

[17] See Laurie M. Johnson Bagby, "The Use and Abuse of Thucydides in International Relations," *International Organization* 48, no. 1 (Winter 1994): 133, https://doi.org/10.1017/S0020818300000849.

[18] Colin S. Gray, "British and American Strategic Culture" (unpublished paper prepared for the Jamestown Symposium, 18–19 April 2007).

[19] Snyder, *The Soviet Strategic Culture*, 5.

> *adapting to the environment and solving problems with respect to the threat or use of force.*[20]

These early attempts at defining strategic culture hinted at the challenges the concept is to face in the coming years, as the definitions seemed all too inclusive and expansive. Similarly, Gray, an enthusiastic proponent of the concept, embraces an earlier attempt by Snyder, which defined strategic culture as

> *the sum total of ideas, conditioned emotional responses, and patterns of habitual behavior that members of a national strategic community have acquired through instruction or imitation and share with each other with regard to strategy.*[21]

Though Snyder's definition refers to a state's cultural characteristics, it provides no guidance as to which of them should be the focus of study or how to solve the issue of having contradictory cultural tendencies. Snyder and Gray, however, identify the members of the national strategic community as the group whose cultural characteristics should be the focus of inquiry. However, while Gray points out the discrete group that bears the characteristics associated with strategic culture, his definition's reference to the "sum total" of cultural elements that poses a dilemma for any researcher—either include any and all cultural elements or select those deemed to matter in an individual case study.

Many authors also adopt a working definition of strategic culture and apply it to specific case studies. For example, Jeannie L. Johnson, with an eye on methodological issues, is more concerned with how a definition will guide the research for specific case studies:

---

[20] Ken Booth, *Strategy and Ethnocentrism* (New York: Holmes & Meier Publishers, 1979), 121.

[21] Snyder, *The Soviet Strategic Culture*, 8.

Strategic culture is the set of shared beliefs, assumptions, and modes of behavior, derived from common experience and accepted narratives (both oral and written), that shape collective identity and relationships to other groups, and which determine appropriate ends and means for achieving security objectives.[22]

Although the definitions of strategy differ in their emphasis and reveal theoretical challenges with the use of the concept, they all point out to domestic sources of states' behavior in international relations, and more specifically to cultural elements.

This chapter, too, while recognizing the numerous theoretical issues surrounding the concept of strategic culture, is more concerned with how a definition of strategic culture shapes the work of researchers analyzing the role of culture in states' foreign policy behavior. For the purposes of creating a simple model, this chapter defines strategic culture as the set of shared beliefs, assumptions, and patterns of behavior that define the identity of a country's national strategic community and shape its ways, means, and ends for achieving security.

Consequently, the model includes the following variables, which are the most significant tenets of strategic culture: identity, prevalent national assumptions about the way the international system works, interests of the state in the international system and how they should be achieved, and patterns of national behavior in the international system. This model adopts Snyder and Gray's focus on the security elite as the focus of the study, while also embracing the belief of those culturalists who see culture as both shaping the context for state behavior and as a constituent of that behavior.

Although no widely acceptable definition has emerged,

---

[22] Jeannie L. Johnson, *Strategic Culture: Refining the Theoretical Construct* (Fort Belvoir, VA: Defense Threat Reduction Agency Advanced Systems and Concepts Office, 2006), 5.

since the early 1980s, the study of strategic culture has adopted a diverse and broad research agenda concerned with identifying cultural, ideational, and normative factors that may influence the strategy and behavior of the state. Gray makes a powerful case for the use of strategic culture as a tool for understanding the security policies of a state.[23] Every society has a distinctive strategic culture that is the product of historical experience. Every society conducts war and behaves in conflict according to its distinctive character while constrained or empowered by context and circumstances. Societies differ in their beliefs and practices vis-à-vis war, peace, and strategy, and these differences are likely to manifest themselves in policy, strategy, and behavior.

Although there are many limitations to the concept of strategic culture—issues of definitions, methodology, etc.—it is useful to know a state's strategic culture. This knowledge provides insights into how the state perceives the international system; what the state's long-term goals and interests are; who the state traditionally see as friends and foes; what its perceptions of the interests, goals, and intentions of other states are; what options for policies and actions it may consider and what options it may not consider; what explains the state's force posture and structure; how the decisions are made and policies applied; and who are the major players in the decision-making process. Knowledge about the strategic culture of a state may help to distinguish between its more and less likely courses of action and anticipate some second- and third-order effects in the state and its behavior in response to external events.

One of the most important issues in studying a country's strategic culture is one of methodology—identifying the sub-

---

[23] Gray, "British and American Strategic Culture."

jects to be studied and how they can be analyzed.[24] Although there is no universally accepted agreement on this, one of the more popular methodologies was developed by Alastair Iain Johnston, who identified the writings, debates, thoughts, and words from a state's strategists, military leaders, security elite, weapons designs, as well as media images of war, military symbols, and military literature to be among the objects most laden with evidence of the state's strategic culture.[25] Similarly, Gray suggests that culture is to be found in society's ideals, its documents and some other material artifacts and icons, and in its behavior.[26] Other approaches invoke influences from history, geography, ideas, texts, and experiences that have impacted a state's strategic identity. Jeannie L. Johnson identifies value-laden national cultural variables that have an effect on security policies, including identity, values, norms, and perceptive lenses.[27]

Another methodological issue is the question of *whose* strategic culture is the subject of study. Most students in the field simply refer to the state when analyzing strategic culture. However, states do not define goals, make decisions, and act—people do. But who exactly does this—society at large, a small group of policy makers, or a community of individuals involved in thinking and acting strategically? If we want to know the strategic culture of a state, do we discern it in the state at large or instead focus on the national strategic community? The national strategic community includes policy makers in the legislative and executive branch, military leaders, academics, influential public figures, and even the judicial branch of gov-

---

[24] It must be noted that strategic culture is an *approach* rather than an explanatory *theory*. To devise an explanatory theory of strategic culture, it would be necessary to identify the causal process whereby culture is translated into strategic decisions and behaviors.

[25] Johnston, "Thinking about Strategic Culture," 49.

[26] Gray, "British and American Strategic Culture," 8.

[27] Johnson, *Strategic Culture*, 11–14.

ernment involved in the shaping of national security strategies. Modern societies have a heterogeneous nature, and identifying a single strategic culture is challenging. Should we then instead focus on a particular group—the national strategic community, for example—and try to identify its strategic culture? One is tempted to take this route, especially because it seems that the preferences, choices, and behavior related to the security of states reflect the preferences and culture of the elite members of a given society. Yet, there are many examples of elites making choices that contradict the preferences of the society. The security elites of Communist countries in Eastern Europe during the Cold War frequently selected courses of action that seemed to contradict what one would describe as the prevailing preferences of the society at large. Their sudden fall from power in 1989 revealed how inconsistent their choices were with the national strategic culture, as states in the region changed their goals and preferences almost overnight.[28] Although there are no clear solutions to these dilemmas to be found, one must be aware of the potential pitfalls in selecting a particular approach. At a minimum, one must determine whether the preferences and policies of elites are consistent over time with the prevailing preferences and attitudes of the society at large.

The research method proposed consists of a framework including cultural variables that have an effect on a state's security policy and behavior. These include identity, assumptions about the international system, the pursuit of interests in the international system, and patterns of state behavior in the international system. Each variable is associated with a set of research

---

[28] Many authors called this the "return of history" to the region. For a description of how Soviet dominance imposed on Communist countries in Eastern Europe a foreign policy behavior that was a radical departure from existing patterns, see Joseph Rothschild and Nancy M. Wingfield, *Return to Diversity: A Political History of East Central Europe Since World War II*, 3d ed. (New York: Oxford University Press, 2000).

questions (to be found at the end of this chapter) to guide the analysis. This framework operationalizes the working definition by guiding the researcher through a series of questions, but it ultimately allows the researcher the freedom to choose the most important variables associated with their particular case study. This is important because the dynamic nature of culture means that the underlying factors contributing to individual strategic culture will vary.

The Tenets of Strategic Culture

This section of the chapter discusses each of the variables associated with strategic culture. Each variable includes a set of associated research questions to be found at the end of the chapter.

Identity

This chapter refers to identity as a shorthand label for varying constructions of national identity and state identity.[29] Identity is a national ideology of collective distinctiveness and purpose.[30] It defines what makes one state different from all other states. Identity is a self-image of distinctiveness held and projected by the state. It is formed and modified through relations with other states. Identity is crucial in the study of security as

---

[29] See the meaning of identity as used by the authors of essays in Peter J. Katzenstein, ed., *The Culture of National Security: Norms and Identity in World Politics* (New York: Columbia University Press, 1996).

[30] A group of people sharing the same national identity is called a nation. The terms state, nation, and nation-state are often used interchangeably, although there are differences between them. *Nation* refers to a group of people who in addition to sharing a common identity also would like to govern themselves in a separate state. *State* is a legal entity composed of territory, population, and government and is recognized by other states. A *nation-state* is used when the boundaries of the state and the nation are the same. Thus, not all nations have states (e.g., the Palestinian nation), while some states have more than one nation within their borders (e.g., Belgium). Nation-state is also widely used in recognition of the fact that in most cases people living in a state do have a common identity and thus are a nation.

states are concerned with construction of identity through the interplay of differences or distinctions with other states. States try to establish unique national identities that distinguish them from other states to provide a positive sociocultural identity to their citizens. Understanding identity gives us insights into what the state sees as its origin, virtues, foes and friends, and destiny.

A word of caution is in order. Identity exists both at the level of individual identity and collective identity. When this chapter refers to national and state identity, it means the identity framed, promoted, and supported by the state. It might or might not be the dominant identity among the people in the state, but it is the one the state endorses as the dominant identity. The state supports this identity through education, socialization, propaganda, and other means, while discouraging or suppressing alternative ideas about national identity.

Although states almost invariably claim to have the origins of their national identities' in the very distant past, most of them are new constructs, and the study of identity encompasses relatively short historical periods.[31] Whenever their formative period occurred, whether in the distant or recent past, this era is a state's most important period of its evolution, and it is thus also crucial in the study of a state's strategic culture. This period tends to have great impact on identity as symbols, traditions, and narratives from this period are considered beyond national dispute—almost sacred in some states. The national foes in this period tend to remain the national foes; significant aspirations and values associated with that phase usually remain intact into modernity. For example, witness how many in the United States defend the legitimacy of intervention abroad in defense of other democracies with the birth of the Ameri-

---

[31] The state as an entity has existed for thousands of years. The nation, a group of people sharing the same national identity, is a relatively new social construct.

can nation in opposition to undemocratic British oppression. National flags, anthems and symbols, military uniforms and insignia, arts, mass education, and national narratives are all heavily influenced by the formative years of a nation.

Identity also determines whether the nation coincides with the state. If identity is based exclusively on a single ethnicity, it is very likely then that groups outside the state borders that share the same ethnicity would be identified as part of the nation, sometimes known as *irredentism* when territory is attempted to be reclaimed. This is one of the most frequent sources of conflicts in international politics as states seek changes to national borders in order to join ethnic minorities residing in other states to the nation. Knowing whether an identity includes not only groups in the state but also minorities beyond the border provides insights into a state's long-term goals and strategies. States may feel a special responsibility for ethnic brethren in other states, which would compel them to interfere in their affairs and cause international conflicts. For example, in 2010, Hungary caused tensions with its neighbors when it allowed ethnic Hungarians living abroad to apply for Hungarian citizenship. The move was perceived as a security threat by Slovakia as close to one-tenth of its population is of Hungarian ethnicity.[32] In retaliation, Slovakia amended its own citizenship law, stripping anyone of their Slovak citizenship if they applied for another citizenship.

Identity also includes the shared values of those belonging to the nation. One may argue that people and groups of people share universal values. For example, Americans frequently argue that people all over the world are not that different, and they value democracy, human rights, and freedom of speech. One can certainly make this case, however, it ignores the fact that nations prioritize and order values differently, and in dif-

---

[32] "Slovaks Retaliate over Hungarian Citizenship Law," BBC, 12 March 2012.

ferent contexts the order may change. Violent conflicts, for example, tend to make security a higher priority than other values. Although values tend to change only slowly, their shifting order may influence the state's behavior in new ways.

When analyzing the state's identity, we must keep in mind that it is not a simple aggregation of the identities of people and groups in the state. In fact, a state may have two or more groups that have different, often competing and conflicting, identities. In this case, what we recognize as the *state identity* may be the identity of the group that holds the monopoly over institutions of the state and its political system. Identifying the existence of more than one identity and assessing their relationships and balance of power provides insights into the stability and durability of the dominant state identity.

Understanding the dynamics between groups' identities also provides insights into a state's ability to prevent violence and conflict among groups in a single state. In some states, groups sharing identities different from the dominant nation may simply want no part in the state. If such groups have the capacity, they may prefer to split from the state and create a new state or join another. Analyzing the relationships of group identities in the state provides an understanding of the strength of dominant identity, the future stability of the country, and some of the domestic forces that shape its international behavior.

This analysis also has significant implications for the Marine Corps, as it provides insights into a state's will to endure in a fight, deploy a cohesive military force, and summon the will to overcome hardships. The more fractured the society in which groups do not share the same national identity, including, among others, ethnic, racial, and cultural attributes, the more difficult it will be for the state to mobilize, deploy, and sustain military power. However, the politics of identity is only one of several factors that influence the state's capacities.

The existence of multiple group identities and even national identities in a state does not in itself suggest a structural weakness, which manifests under certain conditions. What matters is whether there are incompatibilities and conflicts among identities. Having the statistics on the ethnic composition in a state, for example, is just a start. Having an understanding of the dynamics and politics of interethnic relations based on different identities is the next logical step in capturing the complex state of identity and its effects on the strategic culture of the state.

Assumptions about the International System

States have different views of the nature of the international system and how it works. Some states subscribe to the view that the system is inherently conflict and violence prone, war is the rule, and its absence is the exception. In such an environment, the logic follows that states seek to maximize their power as the only way to guarantee their security. Although there are international organizations, such as the UN, which exist for the purpose of settling conflicts and preventing wars, and there is international law created to ameliorate conflicts, these organizations and institutions are often powerless to prevent aggression and provide security. States are on their own when it comes to assuring their survival and interests. Only power can ensure security. In seeking power and security, states may enter into alliances, but there are no permanent friends, and alliances disintegrate once their goals are achieved. Cooperation is always temporary, and once it stops serving the interests of the states, they end it. Even when violence is not likely, dealings between states are a zero-sum game: you either win or lose in dealings with other states.

Other states, although accepting that there are conflicts in the world, many with the potential to turn violent, see the system as more ordered and predictable. These states recognize that there is a mutual benefit in cooperation to create various formal and informal arrangements and institutions to promote conflict resolution and alter the political calculations of other states. Cooperation among the states is not only possible but durable because it is based on a win-win game; all states can benefit from cooperation. Institutions that promote cooperation not only ameliorate and prevent conflicts but also have the capacity to change the state's view of the international system and alter their goals of accumulating power as the ultimate, zero-sum game as a guarantee for survival.

Although these two views represent the two opposite extremes of a continuum, all states fall somewhere in between. The view of the international system is the lens the state uses to interpret events and the policies of other states. It is also the foundation of a state's own policies. These views have strategic and political consequences; they are translated into policies that have real-world consequences. States that ascribe to the first view or one of its variations would seek to maintain large military power even when no immediate enemy is identified, and they would be quicker to resort to violence or the threat of violence than states that do not hold this view. They would also be more prone to switching alliances.

Russia, for example, seems to subscribe to the pessimistic view on the nature of the international system. As indicated in national security documents, Russian security elites believe that states unapologetically seek to accumulate power as the ultimate guarantee for national security and interests.[33] The use of violence is a legitimate instrument of national policy and states readily use it in furthering their interests. Wars occur frequently, and international institutions and law have only a limited ability to ameliorate conflicts between states. In such

---

[33] For an excellent summary of Russia's strategic culture, see Dmitri Trenin, "Russia's Threat Perceptions and Strategic Posture," in *Russian Security Strategy under Putin: U.S. and Russian Perspectives* (Carlisle, PA: Strategic Studies Institute, U.S. Army War College, 2007), 35–47.

a world, states have no choice but to consider states with significant power as potential enemies. Accordingly, states always seek to increase their relative power in anticipation of a conflict with a yet unknown or emerging future enemy. Current partners can always turn into enemies. These are fundamental assumptions that shape the Russian elite's thinking, behavior, and strategies. In other words, these assumptions of this particular state mind-set have policy and political consequences. This outlook prompts Russia to heavily rely on the military and defense posture for its security, seeking to strengthen its capabilities by preparing to face any potential adversaries. In the case of Russia, one may also argue that these fundamental assumptions about the nature of the international system are shared by both elites and the public at large.

Unlike Russia, the United States has a more benign view of the international system. One of the reasons for this difference is that the current international order was actively crafted by the United States and reflects many American preferences. After World War II, the United States emerged as the preeminent world power. While recognizing Soviet dominance in parts of Asia and Europe, the United States also embarked on crafting a liberal world order based on institutions, alliances, norms, and practices that reflected American values and interests.[34] The goal of this international order was to stabilize international politics, safeguard American security and its way of life, and advance American interests worldwide. More specifically, it included institutions and norms that promoted free trade, financial stability, political integration among states, conflict resolution, and democracy and human rights. American values and norms shaped the international order that emerged after the war. The Soviet Union, although a participant in the

---

[34] Michael J. Mazarr et al., *Understanding the Current International Order* (Santa Monica, CA: Rand, 2016), https://doi.org/10.7249/RR1598.

creation of the post–World War II order, created a sphere of influence—with its own political, economic, and social foundations—that differed markedly by the one created by the United States and its allies. The end of the Cold War left the Soviet order in ruins and the American order intact.

Getting to know a state's fundamental assumptions about the international system is a crucial step, as it provides a powerful tool in understanding the state's perceptions and behavior, which would help avoid actions that may be misconstrued by its decision makers. Russia's behavior and perceptions, once again, provides a good case in point. The expansion of NATO into Eastern Europe in 1999–2004 was seen by the West as a natural enlargement, which included states that aspired to become part of the Euro-Atlantic community and, at least from the American point of view, presented no threat to Russia. Russian elites, and later the Russian public, however, saw this process very differently. Although NATO was seen as presenting no immediate security threat to Russia, Russians perceived the expansion as, among other things, a long-term threat to its territory and interests. By the Russians, it was perceived as an encroachment of a powerful military alliance on Russian borders and spheres of influence. Similarly, U.S. attempts in the 2000s to place components of a defense shield against Iranian missiles in Eastern Europe were perceived as a direct threat to Russian security. In Russia's thinking, it was the availability of foreign military capabilities near the borders that mattered, not the rationale and intentions of the foreign power that deployed them.

Discerning where the state stands on the nature of the international system continuum can be tricky. Today, even pessimistic states commend the virtues of cooperation and international law.[35] However, they also share a deep-seated distrust of cooperation, international law, and institutions as a solution to their security dilemmas and challenges. Only careful reading of statements by members of the security elite and the wording of national security documents can reveal a state's dominant assumptions and attitudes regarding the nature of the international system.

The Pursuit of National Interests in the System

Identity and how the state sees the international system heavily influences the way the state defines its role or interests in the system and how to pursue those interests. Societies tend to have narratives—sometimes more than one, even competing ones—about a state's aspirations and role in the world. In the past, political leaders and elites used to speak of a state or a nation's destiny; Manifest Destiny is one American example. Examples from various states and times include the spread of civilization (as defined by the state spearheading the effort), the spread of Christianity or another religion, or the enlargement of the living space for a nation. The system, ranging from the entire international system to the small regional system, was seen as imperfect and required the efforts of the entire state to correct. More recently, states tend to list their vital interest and goals in formal documents, including national strategies, national doctrines, and security strategies. Depictions of national purpose and interest also find their way into speeches and articles by political leaders and representatives of the political and nonpolitical elites.

Knowledge about what the state sees as its place in the system and how to achieve it reveals two important understandings. First, states either accept the fundamental order

[35] Louis Henkin, *How Nations Behave: Law and Foreign Policy* (New York: Columbia University Press, for the Council on Foreign Relations, 1968).

of the international system or they reject it either entirely or partially. The modern international system, which is based on nation-states; a system of international organizations, including the United Nations, International Monetary Fund, the World Bank, World Trade Organization, and various regional organizations; the principles of free trade, free flow of capital, and the freedom of the commons; and the almost universal acceptance, if not practice, of democratic governance and human rights—is carefully maintained by states and international organizations. The system is what it is because the influential states in it, particularly the United States with its enormous military and financial might after the Second World War, had crafted it and maintain it. Most states accept the fundamental principles of this order and do not seek to change it.

There are states, however, who see the system as fundamentally unjust and contrary to their strategic goals and interests. The Soviet Union during the Cold War, for example, although a member of the United Nations, created an alternative international Communist system that had very different values, norms, and beliefs and sought to spread it throughout the world. Moscow participated in the United Nations because it was a useful venue to play power politics in the bipolar struggle with the United States, and it had a particularly strong influence on the organization as a permanent member of the UN Security Council. However, it rejected participation in almost all other institutions and practices of the international system outside the UN. The Soviet Union and its allies were not members of the World Bank, the International Monetary Fund, the World Trade Organization (known as the General Agreement on Tariffs and Trade during the Cold War), did not practice free trade, and accepted intervention in one another's affairs when the Communist nature of the regime of any state was under threat, including internal threats. Above all, the Communist states sought a fundamental change to the international system. If the Soviet Union had won the Cold War, the current international system would look very different and would reflect their strategic interests.

Other states, too, can find the existing international system unjust on a regional level and take steps to change it. Iran, for example, sees the international order in the Persian Gulf and the Middle East as unacceptable and makes no secret of its willingness to change it. In the past, Germany, after the First World War, rejected the peace settlement that carved out German territories and denied the state what it perceived as its rightful place as a great European power. This rejection was eventually translated into policies to remake the existing order and led in part to the Second World War.

Two potential ways to describe how states pursue national interests include status quo and revisionism. States that accept the existing international order and do not make attempts to change it fundamentally are called *status quo states*. Conversely, states that do not accept the existing order and seek to remake it are called *revisionist states*.[36] Not all states that reject the existing regional or international order take steps to remake it, as this action in most cases requires capabilities beyond what is available to them and risks opposition from many states.

Even when states do not seek to change the system, their self-declared goals and interests reveal important information about what drives their policies and actions. Of course, the behavior of the states is determined not only by intentions but also by material factors. Still, the self-declared goals of the state, coupled with what it possesses as capabilities to achieve its goals and the international context and distribution of pow-

---

[36] Jason W. Davidson, *The Origins of Revisionist and Status-Quo States* (New York: Palgrave Macmillan, 2006).

er at the time, provides clues about whether certain actions are possible or likely.

Most states do not hide their fundamental interests and goals. They are signaled not only to the outside world but are also a powerful instrument in garnering domestic support and mobilizing the public. One must always consider whether there are discrepancies between the proclaimed interests and objective of the state's elite and the interests and objectives of the society and its groups. For example, the Communist elite of East Germany aligned its policies, including its foreign policy, with those of the Soviet Union. The society in East Germany, however, did not generally align ideologically and culturally with the Soviet Union but rather with their compatriots to the west.

Patterns of State Behavior in the International System

Strategic culture may have a powerful effect on how states behave, or it may have a very limited effect. In different contexts and circumstances, a variety of factors influence the decisions and policies of leaders, including noncultural factors such as material capabilities, geography, and institutional constraints and opportunities. Discerning patterns of behavior and assessing them against what we have identified as elements of the nation's strategic culture from official documents, national narratives, and symbols would help identify how strong the relationship between the state's strategic culture and its behavior is. At the same time, we must be aware that the state's pattern of behavior is part of its strategic culture. For example, Gray's argument is that strategic culture must be seen as *shaping* behavior and itself is a constituent of that behavior.

Knowing the strategic culture of a state does not necessarily enable us to predict the behavior of the state under different circumstances. In determining state behavior, sometimes strategic culture matters more, sometimes less. For example, the strategic culture of the security elite may favor the use of force in a particular case. However, the capability of the state to mobilize forces may be limited by the inability of the armed forces to mobilize on short notice, an international environment unfavorable to military options, or geographic and weather conditions that make warfare hard in the short term. In these cases, it may force the decision makers to rule out the use of force as a preferred course of action. Similarly, crises have the capacity to reveal the true nature of strategic culture of a state as security leaders. The lack of time to respond, coupled with high stress, tend to force states to fall back on patterns of behavior, while at the same time demonstrating incongruities in strategic cultures, as the lack of time and the high stress tend to lead to misperceptions, miscalculations, and counterproductive decisions.[37]

Considerations When Researching Strategic Culture

The type of political system is an important consideration when researching strategic culture. The national political system does have an effect on the strategic culture of the state. Political leaders in democracies, for example, face complex decision-making and implementation processes. When they formulate the policies of their states and make decisions, they need to take into consideration multiple institutions and players that have authorities and responsibilities in the decision-making process, including the public (whose support the leaders need), the legislative and judiciary branches of government, and various interest groups.

In contrast, leaders in nondemocratic states face fewer political and institutional constraints. Operating in a nontransparent and nonaccountable environment does not mean that

---

[37] Robert Jervis, *Perceptions and Misperceptions in International Politics* (Princeton, NJ: Princeton University Press, 1976).

leaders of undemocratic societies do not carefully weigh various possible courses of action. It means, however, that there are fewer checks on the decision-making process, as power and authority are concentrated in a single institution or a single leader, which makes the decision to use force or the threat to use force contingent on the whims of relatively few people. Such leaders do not have to include in their calculations institutional and public opinion support. They can easily mobilize military forces without seeking formal approval from national institutions, including legislative approval for the use of force and appropriation of financial resources. Quantitative and qualitative anthropological studies support the hypothesis that societies and groups with widespread participation in decision making and higher elite accountability are less prone to war, while societies characterized with less leadership accountability and more hierarchy are more war prone.[38]

Lack of democracy and transparency in the political system also makes the study of strategic culture difficult. While the decision-making process and the players in it are transparent in democracies, it is hard for the outside observer to discern the organizational culture of a nondemocratic state, including who is in charge of the process and how it works. In addition, nondemocracies rarely declare their long-term security goals and the means to achieve them in official, formal documents such as national strategy, military and defense doctrines, defense reviews, or white papers. These states also discourage the emergence of independent think tanks and institutes that might conduct research on security and defense and publish their findings. Instead, the researcher has to rely on limited information and indirect evidence. For example, when a coun-

---

[38] Jack Snyder, "Anarchy and Culture: Insights from Anthropology of War," *International Organization* 56, no. 1 (Winter 2002): 23, https://doi.org/10.1162/002081802753485124.

try publishes no official documents on its strategic and security outlook and policies, including real accounting of defense spending, one must look at patterns of behavior and how the country has acted in the past, then draw some conclusions as to how it may act in the future.[39]

Democratic political systems not only impose institutional checks and balances that constrain and enable decision makers, but they also change culture. There are examples where emerging democratic institutions and habits change the very nature of strategic culture. West Germany and Japan after the Second World War introduced democratic institutions and quickly transformed strategic cultures, which previously compelled the states to seek territorial expansion and easily resorted to the use of force, into cultures that can now be defined as pacifist. This pacifism was rooted in democratic institutions and democratic political culture. By creating a political system based on the division of power, more so in Germany than in Japan, the two countries made it virtually impossible for a national government to unilaterally involve the state in a war beyond the national borders. The Japanese constitution prohibited the country from maintaining armed forces: Japan has a Self-Defense Force (SDF) rather than a traditional armed force and the law imposes strict civilian control over the SDF. The German constitution, known as the Basic Law for the Federal Republic of Germany, describes the armed forces as absolutely defensive ones and imposes civilian and democratic control over them. In addition to the structural constraints on the use of force in both countries, the political and social culture makes it very difficult for governments to use the armed forces. Rooted in the pre-1945 period, a culture emerged that not only

---

[39] Gordon G. Chang, "Why China's Military Budget Is Larger than It Appears," *National Interest*, 8 March 2017.

denounced the use of force by both countries but also was generally resistant to the use of force by any country in the world.

These structural and cultural constraints on the use of force in both countries presented a problem after the end of the Cold War when the international community faced a new set of security challenges, and the demands on both countries to contribute to international efforts, including with armed force, mounted. Both countries have adjusted their policies, including constitutionally and institutionally, and now send troops abroad. The strategic cultures of both Japan and Germany, however, are adjusting only slowly and both countries still exhibit passionate internal debates on the legitimacy of the use force abroad. In fact, the examples of Japan and Germany clearly illustrate how knowing the strategic culture of a country provides insights into the constraints an American ally might face when participating in a coalition with the U.S. armed forces. For example, the German forces taking part in the International Security Assistance Force (ISAF) have a mission constrained by multiple caveats that prevent the forces from participation in combat operations. Although the German military has powerful capabilities, strategic culture partially explains why those capabilities cannot be deployed in Afghanistan.

Even democracies have varying institutional structures and decision-making procedures for defining their policies and behavior in the international system. Some states have trusted prime ministers and their cabinets with most of the authorities in this area, while others have vested their presidents with foreign policy and defense powers. In some states, relatively few institutions are involved in the process, and others include multiple institutions, the public, and interest groups. Getting to know the political system and the place of the foreign policy and defense apparatus provides insights into who the most significant players are and how they reach decisions.

Strategic culture can change; however, change is slow and

incremental.[40] Changes in the state's policies and behavior do not necessarily reflect changes in the state's strategic culture. When a state elects a new government, the new administration may adopt policies and behavior reflecting the priorities of the political party running the government. This does not necessarily mean that the strategic culture of the country has shifted. Strategic culture is only one factor that determines the strategy, policies, and behavior of states. There are numerous other factors that have influenced the choices and decisions of a new government, which consequently leads to the state's altered policies and behavior. For example, a state's more pro-American policies after a new government takes power might reflect the more pro-American attitudes of the new ruling party and a shift in American policies toward the country rather than a fundamental shift in the strategic culture of the country.

Similarly, changes in the rhetoric of security elites and in public attitudes that seem to contradict what is seen as the national strategic culture do not necessarily signify a significant shift. Rhetoric and attitudes are very dynamic and heavily influenced by fast-changing contexts and circumstances. Changes in elite rhetoric may be a matter of political expediency rather than a reflection of deeply held values and interests. Strategic culture should be identified as transformed only when the new approach to strategy becomes embedded in institutions, symbols, organizations, training, and force posture.

The case of Germany's transformation after the Second World War is a good example of a fundamental change in strategic culture. The change took place in a broader West German

---

[40] Gregory Giles, for example, points out that demographic and generational changes, media and academic influences, and the rise of individualism and religious nationalism have gradually shifted the foundations of Israeli strategic culture. See Gregory F. Giles, *Continuity and Change in Israel's Strategic Culture* (Fort Belvoir, VA: Defense Threat Reduction Agency Advanced Systems and Concepts Office, 2006).

process of domestic democratization and international integration. Successive West German governments and political and military elites not only adopted democratic rhetoric and antimilitaristic narratives but carefully constructed national institutions that would sustain the democratic foundations of the political order and the overall democratic and civilian control over the armed forces and other security institutions. West Germany also denounced past discredited policies for achieving national goals and instead defined the pursuit of national interests strictly in the framework of an integrated and democratic Europe. For this purpose, the country became one of the main engines of building the institutions of the European Union while it shouldered the substantial financial burden required for this endeavor.

Gradually, a new strategic culture gained a life of its own, distinct from the social and political interests that helped give rise to it. In the past, the use of military force was seen as a legitimate means to achieving national goals (i.e., territorial expansion), but the modern West German state defined its interests in the framework of international (UN, EU, NATO, and the Group of Seven) and domestic (federal states, separation of power, a powerful constitutional court, and civilian control of the military) institutions that constrained any attempt at unilateral pursuits of interests and power. These institutions not only reflected the interests of powerful political and social forces during the emergence of the new West German state, they consequently reinforced and maintained these interests and ultimately transformed the state identity.

Strategic culture is not static. Major events, including the futility of old strategies, generational change, wars, political revolutions, foreign occupation, and other significant developments can spur changes in previously long-held strategic culture ideals. It is therefore prudent to occasionally revisit our knowledge of a country's strategic culture and update the analysis to reflect current situations and political environments.

The Influence of the International Cultural Environment

In addition to the internal cultural environment, the external cultural environment, too, has a powerful influence on states' behavior. As pointed out in the introduction, there are three cultural layers to the international cultural environment in which the states operate—international institutions; patterns of amity and enmity based on culture, ideologies and practices; and world and regional cultural environments. The purpose of this section of the chapter is to demonstrate how the external cultural environment influences and permeates the domestic cultural environment. The concluding section of this chapter includes research questions to assist the study of those influences.

A single example may best illustrate the importance of the international cultural environment. In the current international system, states, frequently with the authorization from the United Nations, intervene in other states to stop human-rights abuses, violence, conflicts between ethnic groups, genocide, and civil wars. In early 2011, for example, after a resolution of the UN Security Council and a resolution of the Arab League, the United States and its NATO allies launched air strikes against the forces of Libyan leader Muammar Gaddafi to prevent them from massacring their political opponents and civilians. This was a foreign intervention in a country based on humanitarian grounds, a type of intervention that is relatively new in international relations.

Until the Second World War, states fought other states, but preventing genocide or stopping the aggression of a government against its people was not one of the causes. The

Second World War spurred a change in the thinking about whether intervening in other states on humanitarian grounds was legitimate and lawful, and gradually states came to accept this as a ground for action. To be sure, the confrontation of the Cold War prevented states from frequently intervening on humanitarian grounds, but in the early 1990s and especially after the civil war in Yugoslavia (1991–95), this became the norm. What happened was a cultural change—what was not permissible at one time now became the norm and the law. One must bear in mind, however, that this international principle is in conflict with another international principle—the sovereignty of the state that prohibits other states from interfering in its affairs. Ultimately, however, the international community accepted that some states, under certain conditions, may lose the protection of sovereignty.

International Institutions

International institutions are important to consider because they have a role in mitigating conflicts. States create international institutions and seek to join them because they facilitate rulemaking, negotiating, implementing decisions, and enforcing rules and decisions. They also help to reduce uncertainty.[41]

International institutions have a significant impact on the national and foreign policies of states. Although institutions cannot eliminate conflict and war between states, they can change the character of the international environment by influencing states' preferences, choices, and policies. International institutions do this by either creating incentives for cooperation or disincentives for particular actions. For example, an international organization can impose trade sanctions on a state and demand changes to its policies as a condition of

---

[41] See, for example, Lisa L. Martin and Beth A. Simmons, eds., *International Institutions: An International Organization Reader* (Cambridge, MA: MIT Press, 2001).

lifting the sanctions. Alternatively, an international institution can encourage a particular behavior in a state by offering the state trade agreements that will benefit it.

International institutions can also operate to encourage a particular collection of norms, rules, and routines rather than formal structures. Instead of motivating states' behaviors through the use of rewards, they instead create an environment of expectations about the proper behavior of the state: the state acts in ways that are consistent with these expectations even when no self-interest is evident. International institutions facilitate the transplantation of norms and rules into the national cultural context either through a process involving pressure on national elites to adopt the new norms and rules, or a process of voluntary adoption. The process can also occur through radical means, including occupation or pursuit of war crimes through The Hague, which entails major cultural changes. For example, the Allied occupation of West Germany after the defeat of Nazi Germany promoted not only radical changes in the political, social, and economic structures of the state but also dramatic cultural changes.[42]

International institutions vary in their influence over states. The presence of an international institution does not guarantee a state's compliance; therefore, an analyst must research the level of institutional impact. Some have a profound effect on many functions of their members. For example, the European Union, an organization including 28 states, has taken over some of the authorities of its members and set up common policies in areas, including trade, finances, the social sphere, education, and foreign policy—that previously individual states were responsible for. There is also no border control between most of the members of the European Union due to

---

[42] See Thomas U. Berger, "Norms, Identity, and National Security in Germany and Japan," in *The Culture of National Security: Norms and Identities*, ed. Peter J. Katzenstein (New York: Columbia University Press, 1996), 317–56.

the Schengen Agreement (1995) and most of them use a single currency, the Euro. The EU has a profound effect on its members as they now craft common EU policies on various issues based on consensus rather than 28 individual policies.

Other international institutions have much more limited functions and ability to change the policies of their members. Some of them exist for the purpose of addressing a single issue and have rather limited authorities. Others, while possessing limited authorities, have more ambitious missions but rely on simply promoting policies and coordinating the efforts of its members. The United Nations Educational, Scientific, and Cultural Organization (UNESCO), for example, works to "create the conditions for dialogue among civilizations, cultures and peoples, based upon respect for commonly shared values." However, the organization has no authority to force its members to do anything.[43]

A defense alliance, while created to address a single issue —a military threat—is a powerful instrument in creating common security and defense policies among its members. However, once the threat that had prompted the creation of the alliance is gone, the rationale for its existence is also not as relevant.[44]

Therefore, analyzing the cultural effect of membership in an international organization on the state requires an understanding of the nature of this organization. Membership in some organizations, such as the EU, leads to profound changes in the state's preferences, policies, and behavior, while others have rather limited, if any, effects. Fortunately for analysts, this is not a question they need to figure out on their own, as the existing literature on international organizations extensively

---

[43] "Introducing UNESCO: What We Are," UNESCO.org, 2017.
[44] The North Atlantic Treaty Organization (NATO) is an exception to this pattern. After the disintegration of the Soviet Union and the Communist bloc, NATO somewhat redefined its roles and missions and continued to exist.

discusses the institutional and cultural implications on member states. Knowledge of these provides insights into what are possible, preferable, and likely choices and policies for a given state.

Patterns of Amity and Enmity
Based on Cultures, Ideologies, and Practices

Culture, ideology, and practices can determine how states interact. Sometimes similarities in political systems between states help them have harmonious relations, and sometimes they do not. For example, social science research points out that stable democracies are unlikely to engage in violent conflict with other democracies or to let disputes among them escalate into wars. This phenomenon is known in the social science literature as "democratic peace."[45] The research points out that it is not the similarity in the form of government that causes the peaceful coexistence of democratic states—there are plenty of examples of violent conflicts between Communist states or between states ruled by military regimes—but rather the form of government itself. There are both cultural and institutional explanations for this phenomenon.[46]

The cultural explanation for how the form of government influences strategic culture emphasizes the rule of law, individual freedoms and rights, tolerance of dissent, shifting political and social coalitions, and peaceful resolutions of conflicts among groups and individuals in the society as values and attitudes that translate into state values and attitudes. In other words, the political culture of the state aligns with the political culture of its society. Similarly, a society that espouses these values tends to develop affinities with societies that share those

---

[45] For review of the vast literature on democratic peace, see James Lee Ray, "Does Democracy Cause Peace?," *Annual Review of Political Science*, no. 1 (1998): 27–46, https://doi.org/10.1146/annurev.polisci.1.1.27.

[46] Michael W. Doyle, *Liberal Peace: Selected Essays* (New York: Routledge, 2012).

same values and this shared worldview prevents the emergence of enemy images that are essential in initiating or sustaining aggression. Even when conflicts between two states whose societies seem to share these values emerge, as they often do, there is the expectation on both sides that the disagreements would be resolved peacefully, in the tradition of both societies. By contrast, these considerations do not apply when the conflict is between two states governed by two different political systems. The society in the democratic state sees the ruling elite of the nondemocratic states as oppressive and nonrepresentative of the society they govern; in other words, it is illegitimate. The use of force against nondemocratic states is then seen not as a war against its people but against an illegitimate government that oppresses its people.

The structural explanation emphasizes the existence of democratic institutions based on the division of powers, multiple institutions responsible for defense and security policy, regular elections, and multiple checks and balances. These factors make the use of force or the threat of use of force in most cases possible only after careful consideration of options, deliberations among institutions, debate in the society, and multiple inputs in the decision-making process. Leaders must convince other institutions and the public in general that the use of force is the right option. Failure to do so might not prevent them from initiating the use of force. However, the lack of institutional and public support denies them the ability to sustain the effort in the long term. This does not imply that sharing the same ideology and political system assures good relations between states. There are plenty of examples of the opposite. However, democracies seem to be unique in this regard.

There are other similarities in culture, ideology, and practices that may promote amity. Religion, ethnicity, nationality, political ideology, and common historical experience often—but not always—facilitate cooperation between states. The existence of these similarities does not guarantee cooperation between the states sharing it. However, under certain conditions, it may. Looking back at the historical record should identify those conditions. Certain contexts and circumstances reinforce certain traits and elements in identities, for example, and that may prompt two states to seek closer cooperation. Conversely, different sets of contexts may lead to a breakdown in cooperation between states. In any event, history provides the best guide in identifying those patterns. For example, does the country tend to ally with certain states based on specific commonalities? Otherwise, based on what kinds of conflicts does the state tend to confront some states? Relations with other states, of course, do not have to be defined by the use of force or the threat of use of force. Identifying a pattern of intensive political, economic, and social interaction between states tells us something about the effects this pattern may have on each participant.

Regional Cultural Environments

In addition to a global cultural environment, it is possible to delineate regional cultural environments. A set of values, norms, and practices broadly shared by the states in one region may differ from the ones in another region. For example, the understanding and practice of sovereignty and statehood in most of Africa differs from that in other regions. In African states, national identities do not broadly overlap with national borders and formal sovereignty is more important than the real exercise of sovereignty.[47] On the contrary, Europe, particularly the European Union, is experiencing a dramatic change in the understanding and practice of sovereignty as states have

---

[47] Robert H. Jackson and Carl G. Rosberg, "Why Africa's Weak States Persist: The Empirical and the Juridical in Statehood," *World Politics* 35, no. 1 (October 1982): 1–24, https://doi.org/10.2307/2010277.

voluntarily given up many of their authorities and powers and instead entrusted them to supranational institutions. These are not simply institutional changes but fundamental cultural changes that have powerful effects on states, societies, groups, and individual citizens.

In the international system, states and their fates are inextricably tied together, and they are interdependent. *Interdependence* in the international system refers to situations characterized by reciprocal effects among states or among actors in different states. These effects result from international transactions—flow of capital, goods, people, information, and ideas across national borders. These transactions increase almost every year and lead to growing interdependence among states. Developments and events in one state have unavoidable effects in other states. These cause repercussions that have both benefits and costs, depending on the country and the context.

The economic collapse in Southeast Asia in the late 1990s, for example, resulted in dramatic decline in economic activity in this part of the world, which pushed the global demand for energy down. As a result, the price of oil in the global market declined dramatically and motorists in many places in the United States were able to purchase gasoline for less than a U.S. dollar per gallon. The eradication of poppy fields in Afghanistan after the invasion in 2001 not only affected the lives and livelihood of Afghan farmers—a consequence now fully understood by ISAF—but also increased the price of illegal drugs on the market in Western Europe. In the international system, actions and processes have expanding consequences; these actions ripple through the international system because of the interdependent relationships that link the states and their societies.

The consequences of interdependence can be intended and unintended. The spread of revolutions in the countries of the

Middle East in early 2011, for example, increased the uncertainty about the flow of oil to the international market and increased its price—clearly an unintended consequence of the occurrences. Others are fully intended, such as when a diplomatic conflict in 2010 between China and Japan about disputed islands, known as the Senkaku in Japan and the Diaoyu in China, resulted in a Chinese decision to limit the export of rare earth minerals to Japan, which are essential components in various products in cars, computers, and smart bombs.[48] China hoped to punish Japan for its diplomatic position. As the largest exporter of rare earth minerals, China's move increased their price (perhaps another intended consequence) but also forced other countries to seek alternative sources of the minerals, including in places where the extraction was previously unable to compete with the Chinese prices (perhaps an unintended consequence of China's decision).

International interdependence has two important dimensions. First, states are sensitive in various degrees to changes in the international system and the behavior of actors in it. The degree of sensitivity depends on how quickly a state is affected by changes in the other states or the international system. The quicker the change is felt, the more sensitive to interdependence the state is. Second, states are vulnerable—to various degrees—to changes in the system. The higher the cost of change on a state imposed by developments in the international system, the more vulnerable the state. For example, some oil-producing states that rely exclusively on the export of oil for their income are not only sensitive to the changes of global prices of oil but also very vulnerable to those changes, particularly in comparison to oil-producing states that have more diversified economies—their national income is not as severely

---

[48] Keith Bradsher, "Amid Tensions, China Blocks Vital Exports to Japan," *New York Times*, 22 September 2010.

impacted by the fluctuation of a single commodity. In general, the states that are both highly sensitive and highly vulnerable to interdependence are prone to instability and turmoil.

States are also unequally interdependent. A relationship of asymmetrical interdependence between two states characterizes a relationship in which one state is more dependent on the other, while the latter is less. For example, the economic relationship between the United States and Mexico is one of interdependence. However, Mexico's economic development is much more dependent on the health of the American economy than the other way around. An economic crisis in the United States would have more serious negative consequences for the Mexican economy than a crisis in the Mexican economy would have on the U.S. market. This logic applies in security and defense as well. For example, during the Cold War, Western Europe depended much more on the U.S. commitment to defend it in case of a Soviet attack, while the United States relied less on Western Europe to face the Soviet threat. Yet, the security interdependence between Western Europe and the United States was beneficial to both sides.

Current interdependence is characterized by a higher degree of sensitivity and vulnerability than in the past. In response to these conditions, states develop various strategies to address national sensitivities and vulnerabilities. Yet, some states are more capable than others of doing so. The more successful states—recognizing that the modern world is truly interdependent and sensitivity to changes is impossible to avoid, short of imposing complete self-isolation—develop strategies and policies to address vulnerability. States that rely exclusively on imports to meet their energy needs, for example, are aware that they are both sensitive and vulnerable to changes in the price and availability of energy sources on the world market. To address their vulnerability, they may attempt to diversify the sources and the types of energy commodities they import, while at the same time they might take steps to limit their dependence on energy imports by developing domestic sources of energy.

Nonetheless, putting these policies in place and changing the trends is challenged by the power and pace of the forces of interdependence. Even powerful states have a difficult time diminishing vulnerability—witness the United States' growing dependence on imported oil for its energy needs, despite often-declared goals of gaining energy independence. Weak and poor states have an even harder time. The food prices on the global market increased substantially in 2009–10 and triggered crises in poor countries that are both sensitive—in that they rely on constant foodstuff imports for their needs—and vulnerable because they do not have the financial resources to purchase imports due to increasing food prices.

Assessing a country's sensitivities and vulnerabilities in today's interdependent world provides further understanding of a state and its people. It must be noted that this assessment must include not only the effects of interdependence on the state but also on its institutions, society, and diverse groups. Not all groups in the society are equally sensitive and vulnerable to changes and events outside the state. In assessing the repercussions to states from changes in the international system, one must carefully identify what groups (e.g., industries or institutions) in the state will be most affected before proceeding to assess the overall effect on the state as a whole. Only then may one proceed to make an informed speculation about the possible responses and behavior by the state, its institutions, society, and its diverse groups. Interdependence is also very dynamic; states and groups in it respond to changes in the international environment by adopting policies designed to maximize benefits from changes and minimize negative consequences—a process that triggers another set of events, changes, and aftereffects.

Conclusion

A systematic approach to researching strategic culture will help analysts better understand the countries and regional and global contexts they are studying. This chapter does not help to predict what the behavior of a state is going to be under different conditions; rather, it is a guide to getting to know a country better and how it interacts within its ever-changing global and local environment. This chapter advocates thinking about factors other than material capabilities and assets, which are the factors usually considered by traditional security and defense approaches in analyzing countries and regions. Analysts should be encouraged to consider the intangibles, about how cultural factors affect states as actors in the international system, and about the cultural dimension in the interaction between states and their international and regional environments.

Knowing the material characteristics of countries and regions is important. Assessing the size of a country's geographical area, population, economy, military capabilities, and organizations is necessary to evaluate the country and its ability to face various security and defense challenges. However, this analysis will be incomplete, because while evaluating the tangibles, it leaves out some very important intangibles. The strategies, policies, and behavior of the states, and ultimately the outcome of dealings with other players in the international system, depend on some powerful intangibles, including culture. A country may have a large military and advanced weapon systems. However, this does not necessarily translate into a powerful and capable military power and into a national capability to achieve its goals in the international system. If, for example, the population is divided between groups with competing identities—for example, a large group in the country may want to split from the state—this conflict will inevitably influence the cohesion and effectiveness of the armed forces and degrade the country's ability to reach its international goals. And even if the military is cohesive and powerful, the country may not be able to achieve its goals through force if the regional cultural environment makes it unacceptable and politically costly to attain national goals through the use of force. The study of states and regions requires not only analysis of material factors but also cultural and other tangible features.

POSTSCRIPT
Guiding Research Questions for the Analyst

Domestic Cultural Environment
Identity

- Did the state emerge while in a struggle with other political entities (e.g., a colonial power, empire, or dominant state)?
- Does the state incorporate in its symbols, national narratives, and educational systems any memories and histories of rivalries during the formative years of the state? What are the foes in these national struggles? Are the current foes the same as the ones during the formative years of the state?
- Is the national identity explicitly formed in rejection of another state or a group?
- Is any other state seen as having provided help in the formative years of the nation?
- How much of the struggles in the formative years of the state are depicted in the national narrative, education, and arts?
- Is there a single national identity or multiple groups having different national identities in the states? Are there conflicting identities? Is there a history of violent conflict between these groups?
- Is there a group in the state that does not share the same national identity as the state and would like to either break up the state or join another state?
- Are there any groups with identities that are incompatible with the prevailing national identity? Have they been in conflict in the past? Are these conflicts capable of breaking up the state?

- What factors in the past have been capable of shifting and changing the national identity?

Assumptions about the International System

- Where does the nation stand on the nature of the international system continuum?
- Does the state see relations with other states as a zero-sum game or a win-win game?
- Does the nation see cooperation as possible but temporary or does it see it as desirable and mutually beneficial?
- Does the state see wars as unavoidable events or aberrations that can be limited?
- Does the state see military power as the ultimate guarantee for security or does the state see the expansion of international organizations and law as the ultimate solution to interstate wars?

The Pursuit of National Interests in the System

- What has the state identified as its vital interests and long-term goals in official documents?
- Are these official interests and goals shared by the society at large?
- Does the state see the international and/or regional system as fundamentally just or unjust?
- Is the state a revisionist state or a status quo state?
- Does the state have a program/strategy to remake the international/regional system?
- Does the state have the capabilities to remake or maintain the existing international and/or regional system?

Patterns of State Behavior in the International System

- Are the state's strategies, policies, and behaviors compatible with the self-declared visions, roles, and goals in the international system? If not, are there any patterns that can be discerned?
- If there are large discrepancies between declared visions and roles, what explains that? Are the reasons for the discrepancies found internally or externally?
- Do discrepancies represent a pattern of their own?

International Cultural Environment

International Institutions

- What international organizations is the state a member of? Which of them have significant impact on the state's behavior in the international system? In what way do memberships in international organizations affect the state's behavior?
- Are international organizations using incentives or penalties to influence the behavior of the state?
- Are there any values, norms, or practices promoted by the international organizations that the state internalizes, which then become the state's values, norms, and practices?
- Are there any elements of the state's foreign, security, and defense policies that are determined or heavily influenced by international organizations (e.g., NATO, EU, Arab League, etc.)?
- Are there cases when the state acts in conformity with the policy of an international organization even if that policy seemed to contradict the state's short-term interests?

Patterns of Amity and Enmity Based on Culture, Ideologies, and Practices

- Are there any patterns of amity and enmity based on culture, ideologies, and practices the state has with other states, groups in other states, international organizations, or transnational players?
- What contexts and circumstances create amity or enmity based on culture, ideology, and practice?
- What are the policy and behavioral consequences of amity or enmity?

Regional Cultural Environments

- Is the regional cultural environment different from the prevailing world cultural environment?
- What are the basic tenets of the regional cultural environment?
- Is the state's strategic culture different from the prevailing regional cultural environment?
- How is the state adjusting to the regional cultural environment?
- How are the world and regional cultural environments affecting the state's sensitivity and vulnerability?
- Does the state have strategies to address various sensitivities and vulnerabilities?

CHAPTER
2

CHINA'S STRATEGIC CULTURE AND ITS DIVERSE STRATEGIC OPTIONS

by Christopher D. Yung, PhD

Introduction

The challenges in assessing the strategic culture of a civilization such as China's are many and varied. The Chinese civilization is one of the oldest on the planet—close to four millennia. Its long history has involved foreign invasions, some of which involved non-Chinese peoples occupying the seats of power in China and then subsequently taking military action against other peoples. It has also had multiple cultural influences: Confucianism, Legalism, Taoism, and Buddhism. Its long history has seen China through many different strategic and military situations. It is a difficult task to generalize across thousands of years of military conflict to arrive at a small set of common cultural factors defining Chinese thinking on strategy.

China has an additional complication when it comes to examining its strategic culture. In addition to its long and varied history, it also had the significant experience of Communism. The Communist experience was so radically different from anything Chinese civilization had experienced before that it can be argued the military thinking and strategies formulated during the Chinese Civil War (1927–37, 1945–49), the Anti-Japanese

War (a.k.a. the Second Sino-Japanese War, 1937–45), and the Cold War should be considered the new foundation for China's strategic culture. During the late nineteenth century, Chinese thinkers, strategists, and government officials found themselves in a hostile, predatory world illustrated by the imperialist powers carving China up into colonial spheres of control. The Chinese civilization was unalterably marked by such a searing experience that some observers argue that if Chinese strategic culture was not realist before, then it certainly became hyperrealist thereafter.[1] This is not to say that pre-Communist strategic thought was necessarily less realist than Communist strategic thought—only that Communist realpolitik behavior is clearly the result of a predatory environment of the late nineteenth and early twentieth centuries. Ancient Chinese strategic thought had many influences, including warlike and unstable interstate conditions. In any case, sinologists have found too many examples of ancient culture having an effect on the way Chinese today think about governance and strategy outside of pure power considerations, and it is safe to say that the characterization of China as a pure realist state is overstated. Thus, it may be that China indeed has a strategic culture, but its historical experiences are so complex that its strategic culture is difficult to identify.

Strategic culture became the subject of study in the late 1990s, with different well-known intellectuals debating complex cases of strategic culture, including China's. For some international relations scholars, such as Colin S. Gray, culture provides a context for understanding decision making instead of identifiable, testable factors. As Gray has written, it is folly

---

[1] In international relations theory, *realism* refers to the concept that countries are power maximizers. They are therefore fixated on measures of power in relation to other nation-states and persistently act to build up their power. This includes the formation of alliances, constant procurement of military equipment, and efforts to threaten and sometimes weaken adversaries or competitors.

to view strategic culture as a means to predict policy behavior or to determine the likely operational or tactical actions of a particular state.[2] Gray notes that there are many factors involved when a country makes strategic and military decisions. Consequently, it becomes conceptually unwieldy for strategic culture as a model for understanding specific strategic decisions to work. At the same time, Gray also correctly observes that strategic culture may help in building a context for us to understand the rationale for strategic and military decisions made by a specific state at a particular time.[3]

Similarly, although Alastair Iain Johnston sparred with Gray for years about the strategic culture issue, he comes to some similar conclusions about the general treatment of strategic culture and what it teaches us about a target country's policy options. He notes that a strategic culture can tell us about the assumptions a country may make about the role of war in human affairs, and it may inform us about that country's view of what strategies have proven effective, given a specific strategic environment. The former emphasizes context and the difficulty of operationalizing the concept of strategic culture; the latter emphasizes the likelihood or probability that a certain type of strategic choice may be preferable to the Chinese under given circumstances. It is probably counterproductive, at least in the case of China, to identify a specific historical incident in China's past and declare it as singularly significant enough to directly lead to subsequent specific strategic decisions. Instead, a civilization's past—in this case China's—can create a background for us to understand how its current leadership may view a variety of specific strategic choices. For this chapter, the complexity of this issue strongly suggests that a different approach is needed to enlighten us on how to think

---

[2] Gray, *Out of the Wilderness.*
[3] Gray, *Out of the Wilderness.*

further about China and how we can apply strategic culture to different societies.

This chapter will take a decidedly different approach to examining this issue. It will first start with strategic issues confronting the modern-day Western strategist and policy maker regarding China, categorize these strategic issues into themes, and then work backward to see if the strategic question involved can be framed and examined in terms of strategic culture. In this way, we can better understand the context in which today's Chinese leadership evaluates their strategic options. By examining several themes in this chapter, it will demonstrate how policy makers and leaders in China prefer to operate as they have within their cultural milieu while adapting to external forces and current strategic challenges. Therefore, at times, it is important to discuss Western ideas on strategy to see how China alternates between its historical preferences and adaptations made to meet these modern, external demands. The goal here is not to provide all-inclusive examples of this tendency but to give readers a better model for understanding Chinese policy behavior.

Confucian, Realist, or Something Else?

The Chinese military and Chinese scholars are fond of the argument that their nation's strategic culture is defensive. As Andrew Scobell notes in his work on this subject, the Chinese are not only inclined to have this view, they are close to fanatical about it. He gives current Chinese strategic thinking the unflattering label of "a cult of the defensive."[4] Scobell notes that the Chinese line of argument is that the foundation of Chinese civilization is Confucian thought. Ideas ascribed to Confucius shaped Chinese views on governance, justice, security, use of

---

[4] Andrew Scobell, *China and Strategic Culture* (Carlisle, PA: Strategic Studies Institute, U.S. Army War College Press, 2002).

force, bureaucracy, the role of government in promoting societal harmony, and commercial policy.

Because Confucius argued that the best policy to preserve peace and harmony, both within China and in territories outside of China, is to treat citizens and neighboring countries justly and to focus on economic prosperity of the society; the Chinese argue that their inclination is to pursue security through policies that are inherently defensive and that pose no threat to anyone.[5] This philosophical line is more than mere academic musing. It has policy implications for the real world. When the U.S. military observes Chinese military modernization, which was based on a 10 percent growth in the Chinese defense budget for close to two decades and the acquisition of very modern weapons systems and platforms, American leaders are inclined to become concerned that China is pursuing a military policy that will ultimately threaten the United States and its national security interests. The Chinese point out that, because their strategic culture is inherently defensive, this is an unfair characterization of China's intentions.

Scobell notes that the Chinese exhibit a curious pattern of fervently believing that their actions and policies are inherently defensive and pose no threat to anyone, yet their actions seem contradictory, reflecting a realist mind-set.[6] Advocates of China as a realist state point to periods in history in which the Chinese authorities acted in un Confucian ways. The earliest evidence of this behavior can be found in the formative years of Chinese civilization. At the end of the Warring States period (403–221 BCE), a single state, Qin, had accumulated enough power to unify the territories that we now recognize as a substantial

---

[5] Scobell, *China and Strategic Culture*.
[6] Scobell, *China and Strategic Culture*.

part of Eastern China.[7] The arguments that the advisors to the Qin ruler gave for unification would be largely familiar to a realist: Qin has the power to unify; the other states have been weakened through years of warfare and are therefore ripe for conquest; and governance of these territories would be much more efficient, just, and effective under unified leadership than under a system of splintered and divided states.[8] Additional historical evidence of realist behavior can be found in battlefield statistics. Some of China's wars cost millions of lives. The Qing military conquest of the Ming in the seventeenth century CE, for example, cost 25 million lives; the Taiping Rebellion of the mid-nineteenth century cost more than 20 million lives; and An Lushan's rebellion during the Tang dynasty in the eighth century CE cost more than 13 million lives.[9] These results suggest that, while Confucian ideas may have had an impact on how the Chinese view themselves and their security as defensive in nature, there is historical evidence that the Chinese in the past have not necessarily adhered to those ideals.

Alastair Iain Johnston's work on Chinese strategic culture is also enlightening. Following a detailed survey of Ming dynasty foreign policy behavior as well as an examination of Chinese Communist military actions during the Chinese Civil War and the Anti-Japanese War, Johnston concludes that China has displayed an unusual reliance on the use of force to settle political disputes.[10] Statistically, Johnston concludes that the modern Communist Chinese use of force exceeds the norm

---

[7] Wm. Theodore de Bary and Irene Bloom, comp., *Sources of Chinese Tradition*, vol. 1, *From Earliest Times to 1600*, 2d ed. (New York: Columbia University Press, 1999), 139–40.

[8] de Bary and Bloom, *Sources of Chinese Tradition*.

[9] Kyle Mizokami, "Asia's 5 Most Lethal Wars of All Time," *National Interest*, 1 August 2015.

[10] Alastair Iain Johnston, "Cultural Realism and Strategy in Maoist China," in *The Culture of National Security: Norms and Identity in World Politics*, ed. Peter Katzenstein (New York: Columbia University Press, 1996), 216–56.

displayed by other major powers. His label for the observed Chinese behavior, a *parabellum strategic culture*, would seem to confirm the views of those analysts who conclude that China is a realist state.[11] Scobell adds in his seminal work on the Chinese use of force that there is a tendency in Chinese culture to decry pacifistic philosophies, and at the same time, to criticize warlike and extremely violent tendencies.[12] He notes that the Chinese philosophical inclination is that force has its place in the world and can be used to bring about just and effective results.[13]

It is here that China's long and complex history becomes instructive. John King Fairbank and Merle Goldman, both historians of China, observe that as early as the Song dynasty, China has had extensive contact through trade with the peoples of Southeast, South, and Middle Asia and was knowledgeable of Mediterranean Europe. They note that China's nautical technology was superior to all of these peoples and had the power to invade and colonize Western Europe from Asia—yet chose not to.[14] The Chinese also correctly note that if China was a realist state, why then did it not continue its expansion? During the Ming dynasty, the Chinese launched seven expeditions throughout Southeast Asia, the Indian Ocean, and parts of the Middle East.[15] Ming-era Chinese military and seafar-

---

[11] A parabellum strategic culture is defined by Johnston as a culture that has an unusual reliance or willingness to use military force to settle political disputes. The country or civilization involved may engage in negotiation and diplomacy as well, however, it also displays throughout its history a tendency to rely on force to resolve major disputes. Johnston, "Cultural Realism and Strategy in Maoist China."

[12] Andrew Scobell, *China's Use of Military Force: Beyond the Great Wall and the Long March* (New York: Cambridge University Press, 2003), 2, https://doi.org/10.1017/CBO9780511510502.

[13] Scobell, *China's Use of Military Force.*

[14] John King Fairbank and Merle Goldman, *China: A New History* (Cambridge, MA: Belknap Press, an imprint of Harvard University Press, 2006), 93.

[15] Charles O. Hucker, *China's Imperial Past: An Introduction to Chinese History and Culture* (Stanford, CA: Stanford University Press, 1975), 291.

ing technology were far superior to any other competitors at that time. China could easily have begun the colonization of the territories ringing the Indian Ocean and the Persian Gulf. There is some dispute about exactly how peaceful these maritime expeditions were, but following the seventh expedition, Zheng He was ordered by the emperor to cease his expeditions, and with the emperor's direction, the nation turned its attention to internal Chinese matters.[16]

China's surprising entry into the modern world in the mid-nineteenth century might have shook Chinese culture to its core. This experience made China prone to realist, power-seeking behavior, at least in the modern era. The Opium Wars, the Sino-Japanese Wars, and later military occupation by Japan left Chinese scholars and government officials seeking solutions to very difficult questions. In the so-called Opium Wars, Western imperial powers forced the opening up of China to trade and colonization, which was eventually followed by the occupation by Japan of the eastern part of mainland China (1937–45). Significantly, Japan had traditionally been seen by the Chinese elite to be China's inferior. These events rocked Chinese perceptions of its historical strength, autonomy, and cultural superiority in Asia.

Out of this context, Mao Zedong emerged as one of those seeking to resolve China's many strategic and political problems. He found his answers in Marxism-Leninism, but his writings also reveal that he found answers in the writings of such military thinkers as Carl von Clausewitz and Antoine-Henri Jomini.[17] This realist narrative goes far in explaining Chinese military and strategic behavior during the Chinese Civil War (1927–37, 1945–49), in its War of Resistance against Japan (1937–45), and in China's strategic behavior during the Cold

---

[16] Hucker, *China's Imperial Past*, 291.
[17] Mao Zedong, "Problems of Strategy in China's Revolutionary War," in *Selected Works of Mao Tse-Tung* (Peking, China: Foreign Language Press, 1967), 1:179–249.

War against not just the United States in Korea but also against the Indians in 1962, the Soviet Union in 1969, and Vietnam in 1979. Following the death of Mao, however, this clean narrative was essentially undercut when Deng Xiaoping came to power in 1979, informed the military that it was to receive little funding for defense modernization, was to be considered the lowest priority for the foreseeable future, and placed the Chinese Communist Party's focus almost entirely on economic growth and enhancing the quality of life of its citizens—a very Confucian notion.[18]

The bottom line is that China is both Confucian and realist in outlook, depending on the specific strategic situation that it finds itself in; China throughout its history has used military force ruthlessly to defeat opponents threatening China's borders and its dynastic rule, but China has also negotiated with nomadic foes living outside of Chinese civilization. Chinese rulers have recognized the utility and necessity of developing military capabilities, particularly new types of weapons; however, at the same time, the Chinese have at the height of their power turned their back on potential conquests outside of the homeland. China has engaged in ruthless wars of annihilation leading to the deaths of millions of combatants, but it has also been involved in multiple conflicts in which lethality and destruction were not what marked the conflict but stratagem and wars of maneuver leading to negotiated outcomes. Chinese strategic culture as described here appears to reflect both a reliance on habits of thought, shared beliefs, and modes of behavior derived from common experiences and narratives during a long period of time, while at the same time reflecting particular ways of adapting to the environment and solving problems with respect to the threat or use of force.

---

[18] Peng Guangqian, "Deng Xiaoping's Strategic Thought," in *Chinese Views of Future Warfare*, ed. Michael Pillsbury (Washington, DC: National Defense University Press, 1997), 3–11.

A Continentalist or Maritime State?

When American strategists look at Chinese military modernization during the past two decades, they worry that China is following directly in the American path toward hegemony. With China's island reclamation activities and its militarization of features in the South China Sea, as well as the apparent emergence of an antiaccess/area denial and counterintervention strategy apparently designed to keep the American military out of the region or, at best, to reduce the U.S. military's room for operational maneuver, they see the emergence of a Chinese version of the Monroe Doctrine against colonialism and designed to ultimately push the United States out of Asia. When American strategists look at the steady development of Chinese naval power projection capabilities, coupled with forays into commercial port facility development in the Indian Ocean and in Africa, they remember the competition the U.S. Navy engaged in with the British Royal Navy in the nineteenth century with the development of American global maritime power. Recent American scholarship backs up this strategic inclination by observing that the father of the modern Chinese People's Liberation Army (PLA) Navy, Admiral Liu Huaqing, initially had in mind plans that were based on the ideas of Alfred Thayer Mahan, America's best-known advocate of early American naval power.[19]

The counterargument is that it is a distortion to use the American model of global power trajectory to assess China's strategic trajectory because, simply put, the United States is not China; the United States attained its hegemonic status in the aftermath of two world wars and the collapse of European colonial powers. More important, while it is evident that Chi-

---

[19] Toshi Yoshihara and James R. Holmes, *Red Star over the Pacific: China's Rise and the Challenge to U.S. Maritime Strategy* (Annapolis: Naval Institute Press, 2013). See also Robert D. Kaplan, *Asia's Cauldron: The South China Sea and the End of a Stable Pacific* (New York: Random House, 2014).

na recognizes the importance of developing a power projection navy and a military capability to protect its interests abroad, China defines its strategic global interests narrowly and does not see the need to militarize its foreign policy so broadly that it ends up being a military competitor with the United States on a global scale. And why does China define its global interests so narrowly? It does so, advocates argue, because China is naturally a continentalist state; views its security and political interests as rooted in what is going on in China proper; and is hyper fixated on security issues that directly affect the legitimacy, survivability, and viability of the government in power.[20] Insofar as international security issues have an impact on those narrow issues, the Chinese government will apply resources and formulate strategies to address them.

The first bit of evidence in favor of one side or the other is historical. For most of China's existence as a polity, its focus has been on the eastern Asian continent and not on the maritime space abutting the Chinese mainland. Chinese history is filled with episodes of dynasties having to wrestle strategically with Turkic, Manchurian, and Mongolian peoples who resided in the steppes, on the periphery of what was considered China proper.[21] Occasionally these nomadic peoples conquered the Chinese state, either through a new military technology (e.g., the crossbow and mounted archery) or because the Chinese state had become corrupt and collapsed from within. These peoples, inevitably convinced that Chinese culture was more refined and superior to their own, were eventually co-opted by the Chinese bureaucracy and absorbed into Chinese culture. These were the experiences of the Mongols and the Manchurians, who became the Yuan and Qing dynasties, respectively.

---

[20] See, for example, Robert Ross, "China's Naval Nationalism: Sources, Prospects and U.S. Response," *International Security* 34, no. 2 (Fall 2009): 46–81.

[21] Mark Elvin, *The Pattern of the Chinese Past: A Social and Economic Interpretation* (Stanford, CA: Stanford University Press, 1973), 26.

Fairbank and Goldman, furthermore, have advanced the thesis that Sinic civilization merged with nomadic peoples to create a polity unique to China.[22] They write:

*(1) . . . [E]arly China created a politicized state organized for purposes of central control both by bureaucratic methods of philosophic persuasion and by the imperial autocrat's use of violence; (2) . . . non-Chinese invaders from Inner Asia became integral participants in the Chinese polity by their military prowess and administrative skill; and (3) . . . the resulting Sino-nomadic imperial power continued to maintain the primacy of central po*litical control.[23]

Additionally, even setting aside the persistent tug of war between Chinese civilization and its nomadic neighbors, the history of the birth, maturation, and collapse of Chinese dynasties resides in the challenges of administering such a vast landmass that the Chinese state encompassed. Mark Elvin, in his classic work, *The Pattern of the Chinese Past*, notes that "the critical factor [in the rise and fall of empires], particularly evident in the . . . early Chinese empires, is usually the heavy cost, relative to total output of food and goods, of maintaining the administrative superstructure, and of providing the soldiers and supplies necessary for imperial security."[24] Inevitably, there is harsh taxation and this in turn tends to induce social and political changes that undermine the fiscal soundness of the state.[25] Fairbank and Goldman describe a similar dynamic:

In each dynasty the progressive withdrawal of land from taxation to benefit the ruling class led to a dangerous

---

[22] For the purposes of this discussion, *Sinic* refers to the cultures of China, Japan, Korea, and Vietnam.

[23] Fairbank and Goldman, *China,* 126–27. Emphasis in original.

[24] Elvin, *The Pattern of the Chinese Past*, 19.

[25] Elvin, *The Pattern of the Chinese Past*, 19.

reduction of imperial revenues. . . . As time went on there ensued a struggle between the interests of the imperial government and of the great families who lived under it.[26]

Wealthy aristocratic families were, over time, able to withdraw land holdings from the reach of imperial power for the purposes of taxation. Additionally, they were also able to convince an increasing number of peasant and middle-income families to stop paying imperial taxes and to come under their protection. "This," according to Elvin, "created a vicious spiral in which a greater burden was placed upon the still-taxable land of the peasantry, at a time when the demands of the government for revenue were probably increasing. . . . [and] a progressively smaller proportion of the land was expected to pay a progressively larger amount of revenue. Peasant disorders would eventually result."[27] These internal issues seem to provide convincing evidence to interpret the Chinese as unvarnished continentalists.

If this pattern of government preoccupation with its internal troubles was the primary concern of those in power throughout Chinese history, it is easy to understand why Chinese rulers may have been inclined to not worry about the maritime domain. The advocates of China as a renewed maritime state point to history as well. They note that perhaps a continentalist perspective dominated Chinese security perspectives in the dynasties previous to that of the Qing dynasty in the nineteenth century; however, by the middle of the century China was confronted with a new kind of adversary—one that came from the sea. The British arrived with modern warships and, unlike previous invasions, did not consider Chinese cul-

---

[26] Fairbank and Goldman, *China*, 48–49.
[27] Fairbank and Goldman, *China*, 48–49.

ture or civilization superior.[28] The British set about forcing the Qing emperor to open China to British trade, to allow British and later other imperial powers to settle in China, and ultimately to proselytize Christianity in China.[29] This century and a half of humiliation that the Chinese readily point to as a primary rationale for a strong navy is evidence that Chinese strategic interests have expanded to include recognition of the importance of a strong navy, as the maritime state advocates argue.

Continentalists claim, however, that history still supports the view that China is culturally more inclined to fixate on continental security issues than maritime ones. They note that the Chinese concern about the sea serving as the domain in which the Western powers invaded mainland China is translated into a naval force structure designed to erect defensive zones to keep outside powers at bay. Antiaccess/area denial as a strategic concept can be interpreted this way; similarly, so can island reclamation and the militarization of island features in the South China Sea. Continentalists also observe that Chinese power projection outside of the Asia-Pacific appears to be, in practice, exactly as they have argued in theory—that is, designed to address narrow security interests that are heavily focused on meeting the direct security needs of the Chinese mainland. China does not build large-scale military bases abroad; rather, it relies on "dual use logistics facilities" that involve a small number of military personnel, do not have the full characteristics of a military base, and cannot be used to fully prepare China for a conventional conflict abroad.[30] Chinese

---

[28] Fairbank and Goldman, *China*, 196.

[29] Fairbank and Goldman, *China*, 196.

[30] Christopher D. Yung and Ross Rustici, with Scott Devary and Jenny Lin, *"Not an Idea We Have to Shun": Chinese Overseas Basing Requirements in the 21st Century* (Washington, DC: Institute for National Strategic Studies, National Defense University, 2014).

military activities abroad have been strictly limited to counterpiracy operations, United Nations peacekeeping operations, noncombatant evacuation operations, and select joint military exercises. Were China a maritime-focused state, it is arguable that these activities would be reflective of actions designed to robustly protect China's expansive maritime policies; instead, they appear to narrowly address specific security interests abroad that are meant to support China's continued economic growth and its internal stability.[31] Again, this brief discussion on China as either continentally focused or maritime focused sheds additional light on the concept of strategic culture. As discussed in the opening chapter of this book, strategic culture is the combination of internal and external influences and experiences—geographic, historical, cultural, economic, political, and military—which shape the way a country understands its relationship to the rest of the world and how that country will behave in the international community.

The "Three Knockheads" of the Tributary System

At the annual Association of Southeast Asian Nations (ASEAN) Regional Forum in 2010, Yang Jiechi, the then-Chinese foreign minister, following an effort by 12 of the ASEAN states to raise the South China Sea territorial dispute as a topic of discussion, turned his ire toward the Singaporean foreign minister, and angrily announced: "China is a big country and other countries are small countries, and that is just a fact!"[32] The angry diatribe reminded many sinologists of the ancient tributary system in which China was so dominant in Asia that the emperor expected smaller kingdoms that were well within China's political

---

[31] Yung and Rustici, *"Not an Idea We Have to Shun."*
[32] Ian Storey, "China's Missteps in Southeast Asia: Less Charm, More Offensive," *China Brief* 10, no. 25 (December 2010).

sphere of influence to make an annual visit to the capital to pay homage.[33] At the beginning of the audience with the emperor, the envoy from the kingdom in question was expected to kneel before the emperor and lower their face to the floor, knocking their forehead three times in supplication. In Chinese, the term is *san ketou* or "three knockheads," hence the phrase in English "kowtow."

The possibility that a long-term goal of China's is to recreate a modern-day tributary system is no laughing matter for scholars who think about foreign policy. If China's political and strategic cultures inherently offer its political leaders the option of demanding an international order that eventually involves Chinese domination with lesser states in constant positions of inferiority, then this is in direct tension with the international order that the United States has created since the Second World War. Even if China's leadership was to press for such an order in the Asia-Pacific region alone, such a structure would be at odds with fundamental American conceptions of its interests in the region. U.S. national security interests have centered on countering the rise of hegemons attempting to dominate their respective regions. In the case of the Asia-Pacific, the United States has a very real interest in maintaining its presence there and to counter an order in which the Chinese leadership expected the surrounding countries of the region to kowtow to Beijing.

Some scholars have observed that the tributary system, when operating under a philosophy of Confucian universal

---

[33] Fairbank and Goldman, *China*, 112, 113, 201.

harmony, led to peace.[34] David C. Kang, in his 2010 book, observed that between the fourteenth and nineteenth centuries China did not engage in war with Japan, Korea, or Vietnam— at the time, the major kingdoms of the East Asian Confucian order.[35] Because states peripheral to China adopted—in one form or another—ideas of the Confucian ethic, which involved a concept of Confucian universal harmony, it is arguable that all of these peoples adhere to a universal or Asian value system.[36] Kang notes that there was no conflict because the four states shared common values in an international system based on a hierarchical structure with China at the top and these countries below.[37]

In contrast to a Westphalian world order in which the ideal is represented by sovereign nation-states in a balance of power with other major states in the system, the Chinese order was hierarchical with the Chinese emperor clearly at the top and with the other nations below. Other scholars have argued that Kang's depiction of East Asian international relations is a distortion of history that cherry-picks supporting facts. Wontack Hong argues that the tributary system was a "glorified pro-

---

[34] The Confucian concept of universal harmony posits that order, peace, and stability are assured when all parties to a political situation, whether they be ruler-subject, a group of civilizations or nation-states, a collection of citizens, etc., have a common set of values and arrive at a common set of governing concepts. Ultimately, this means that peace and order is assured when all parties to a political situation know their place in a hierarchy of political relationships established by a number of different political processes: king-subject, parent-child, merchant-customer, lord-subject, or prosperous state-developing state.

[35] David C. Kang, *East Asia before the West: Five Centuries of Trade and Tribute* (New York: Columbia University Press, 2010).

[36] There is no single definition of an Asian value system. However, common elements of it involve: (1) respect for tradition; (2) a hierarchical view of order and stability, or more specifically acceptance of one's place in a given pecking order; (3) respect for elders and ancestors; (4) a high value placed on education; (5) the prioritization of the welfare of the group or collective over individual interests and rights; and (6) in some Asian societies, an emphasis on stability and order over individual freedoms.

[37] Kang, *East Asia before the West.*

tection racket" in which China shook down those kingdoms weaker than itself while China paid off nomadic peoples along China's steppes, depending on the nature and level of threat these peoples posed to China.[38] A bridge between these two interpretations of the Chinese ancient world order is whether it is the pursuit of harmony or the Chinese inclination to pay off potential threats that provided the motivation for this type of system. The Chinese conception of strategic order comes down to four aspects: (1) a hierarchy of states, each with a clear understanding of their position within the system; (2) a strong sense of values, manifest in ritual behavior to signify compliance with the established order; (3) material exchange as a means to address tension in the system; and (4) the absence of the need to resort to force to maintain order in the system if all of the major players recognize their position in the hierarchy and have well-developed channels to resolve disputes absent the use of force.

Chinese scholars have vigorously argued that China has no desire to return to a tributary system and commentary that suggests otherwise is inaccurate. These scholars, including Yongjin Zhang and Shu Changhe, argue that instead of focusing on the ancient Chinese system demanding tribute, that Western scholars look at the Chinese concept of *universal harmony*, which is really at the heart of how the Chinese tributary system worked.[39] A Chinese notion of harmony as opposed to the Western ideal of balance, Chinese scholars argue, is a more

---

[38] Wontack Hong, *East Asian History: A Tripolar Approach* (Seoul: Kudara International Press, 2010).

[39] Yongjin Zhang, "China and Liberal Hierarchies in Global International Society: Power and Negotiation for Normative Change," *International Affairs* 92, no. 4 (July 2016): 795–816, https://doi.org/10.1111/1468-2346.12652; and Shu Changhe, "The Possibility of Gongsheng International System: How to Build a New Type of Great Power Relations in a Multipolar World," in *A New Type of Great Power Relations: Opportunities and Challenges* (Beijing: Peking University Press, 2015), 81–107.

durable formula for peace. Harmony is based on shared values, while balance, at least in an international relations sense, connotes stasis arising from two opposing forces unable to overcome each other. These scholars observe that the Chinese focus on harmony is pervasive in modern Chinese foreign and defense policy concepts.

The early foreign policy of the People's Republic of China had aspects of the universal harmony theme. Zhou Enlai, China's then-foreign minister, announced in the mid-1950s that the guideline for Chinese foreign policy was the Five Principles of Peaceful Coexistence, known as the Panchsheel Treaty, which came out of the Bandung Conference of 1955. It called for countries to respect the sovereignty of all other nation-states, to not interfere in the internal affairs of other countries, to treat other countries with mutual respect, to not invade and act aggressively toward other nation-states, and to not act like a bullying hegemon.[40]

A recent example of Chinese policy associated with a theme of universal harmony is the larger policy to manage its relationship with the United States, described as a new type of great power relationship.[41] The concept, which originated in 2011, argues that the structural situation China and the United States find themselves in—that is, a rising power, an established hegemon, and an eventual overtaking in global influence of the latter by the former—will likely lead to major power conflict unless something creative is done to manage the relationship. The Chinese concept of a new type of great power relationship is supposed to be that creative solution. In it, the Chinese argue that the United States and China pursue the following path toward an improved relationship: (1) a policy of "no conflict, and

---

[40] Joseph Camilleri, *Chinese Foreign Policy: The Maoist Era and Its Aftermath* (Oxford, UK: Oxford University Press, 1980), 19.
[41] Cheng Li, "A New Type of Major Power Relationship?," Brookings, 26 September 2014.

no confrontation"; (2) mutual respect for each other's "core interests"; and (3) win-win cooperation. American interlocutors engaged in strategic dialogues with their Chinese counterparts wryly observe that the new type of great power relationship is easy to comprehend: all the United States needs to do is respect China's vitally important interests, while China ignores all of America's important interests.

So, does China want to return to a tributary system in the Asia-Pacific or not? If stated another way, does China want to dominate the Asia-Pacific region with China hierarchically on top and other nations of the region below? If this is the question, then the answer is probably "yes." The evidence for this argument can be pieced together through a number of different examples: China's push for an East Asia for Asians to the exclusion of the United States; China's refusal to negotiate or discuss the South China Sea disputes with ASEAN as a unified, coequal body; China's continuing enmity with its most robust regional rival, Japan, even though it would make strategic sense for China to make common cause with the Japanese, if only to ease the United States out of the region; and China's downplaying of South Korea's actual defense needs regarding South Korea's request that the United States deploy a missile defense, known as the Terminal High Altitude Area Defense (THAAD), in South Korea against North Korean missile threats, while China decries the perceived negative effect such a system would have on China's own security needs. The discussion on China's desire to return to a tributary system reinforces some of the conceptual definitions of strategic culture laid out in the opening chapter of this book. In this case, it illustrates how strategic culture refers to the social ordering of the system (either internal to a country, or externally among a number of countries) that individuals rely on to tell them how the world works, which norms and values should be upheld internationally, and which rules should govern state interactions.

Deterrence and Coercion: Two Sides of the Same Coin?

The use of force is an important aspect of strategy, but the associated concepts of deterrence and coercion are understood differently by the Chinese. Westerners, Americans especially, see these concepts as two separate constructs, each with different sets of norms, legal restrictions, accepted actions, and safeguards associated with them. But for China, these two constructs are not considered so distinctly, which causes confusion from those on the outside looking in at Chinese use of deterrence or coercion. To better understand the Chinese point of view, it is first helpful to understand their conceptualizations about power, which are part historical and part linguistic, and equally helpful is a good understanding of China's historical foundations regarding sovereignty.

Essentially, Chinese concepts of sovereignty did not involve the religious, legal, and governmental checks and balances that Western societies accepted or imposed on their rulers. Although developed over centuries, the European system of governance involved kings having to share power over time with religious institutions, such as the Roman Catholic Church, ruling over societies with well-developed systems of law and legal jurisprudence. The Western calculus to use force, then, has traditionally taken into account significant religious and legal factors that invariably demanded a legal and religious justification, and which ultimately involved making a distinction between force designed to defend or retaliate and force designed to compel. By contrast, Chinese emperors did not suffer from similar restrictions on their power and came to develop well-thought-out ideas on how to use military power—either to prevent adversaries or citizens from doing something by deterrence or compelling these same parties to do something through coercive measures.

Arthur Waldron, a keen observer of the connection between Chinese culture and concepts of security, has stated that in China there are different ways to say the word "power."[42] There is *li*, or the attributes associated with power—size of a population; number of men at arms that a ruler has access to; number of ships, weapons, etc.; and the size of the economy. There is *shi*, the skillful use of *li*, and *xing* (the strategic situation or net assessment) to bring about a desired political objective. And then there is *wei*; that is, the appearance of power or awesomeness, which by itself can generate political outcomes because adversaries and friends alike will behave differently around you depending on the degree of *wei* you possess. Of course, the skillful strategist uses *wei* through stratagems to coerce or negotiate a better political outcome for the state. Therefore, in China the ruler was not overly preoccupied with the justification of the use of military power and force, but instead was particularly concerned with the effectiveness of the use of force.

Another distinctive feature of Chinese strategic culture related to deterrence and coercion is the Chinese strategic and philosophic tendency to see political objectives intimately related to the military instrument; notwithstanding Clausewitz's famous dictum, the West does not. When Clausewitz claimed that "war is the continuation of policy by other means," the rejoinder to that phrase was that militaries were to be used to eliminate the armies of one's adversary so that the state can impose its will on the adversary.[43] Clausewitz described militaries as two wrestlers in a ring attempting to gain leverage

---

[42] These concepts were presented during lectures at the U.S. Naval War College in the 1990s. However, the author heard Arthur Waldron make these remarks at conferences on Chinese strategic thinking in the latter part of the 1990s, in particular, a director of the Office of Naval Intelligence-sponsored conference at Lansdowne Conference Center, Leesburg, VA, in June 1996.

[43] Carl von Clausewitz, *On War*, ed. and trans. Peter Paret and Michael Howard (Princeton, NJ: Princeton University Press, 1976), 77, 87.

over the other, the goal of which is to throw and pin the other down.[44] Despite Clausewitz's claim that one was the extension of the other, giving the impression that war and policy making occupied the same conceptual sphere, he commented that ultimately the means through which the military serves the political objective is through combat, so warfighting must be the primary focus of the military. He writes:

> *If a decision by fighting is the basis of all plans and operations, it follows that the enemy can frustrate everything through a successful battle. This occurs not only when the encounter affects an essential factor in our plans but when any victory that is won is of sufficient scope. For every important victory—that is, destruction of opposing forces—reacts on all other possibilities. . . . Thus it is evident that destruction of the enemy forces is always the superior, more effective means, with which others cannot compete.*[45]

Military historian Antulio J. Echevarria II notes that beyond Clausewitzian theory, in practice, the Western strategic tradition is to not view war as a continuation of policy by other means and instead sees it as an alternative to politics. That is, "politics brought war into being, but war existed as a violent alternative to politics, rather than its logical extension."[46] He observes that German, English, French, and American strategists, practitioners, and theorists have tended to use the Napoleonic wars and later Helmuth Karl Bernhard Graf von Moltke's campaigns as the ideal for thinking about wars. For these Western strategic thinkers, "winning wars meant winning battles, and

---

[44] Clausewitz, *On War*, 77, 87.

[45] Clausewitz, *On War*, 97.

[46] Antulio J. Echevarria II, *Toward an American Way of War* (Carlisle, PA: U.S. Army War College Press, 2004), 3.

that doing so would accomplish most, if not all, war time objectives."[47]

This tradition lives on today in the way that Western politicians talk about the use of force. American presidents have said on a wide range of occasions that everything is on the table (i.e., the use of force) but only after we have exhausted every possible solution. The existence of this tradition of the philosophical separation of the political and military spheres was why Americans were so uncomfortable thinking about nuclear weapons. Nuclear weapons are the ultimate political weapon. Their absolute destructiveness limits their utility on the battlefield, and their actual use in the case of a full-scale nuclear exchange would ultimately mean the end of the viability of the states employing them; nuclear weapons are ultimately useless as military weapons but quite as useful as a political weapon to either deter adversaries or to coerce them.

If the Western intellectual tradition tended to separate the political and military spheres, the advent of nuclear weapons forced Western strategic thinkers into fully contemplating the political use of these weapons. Deterrence was suddenly thrust into the policy realm as a central and important guiding defense concept. Preventing aggressive states from violating international law or attacking other weaker states conformed with Western ideas of just war theory and the relationship of force to political order. Coercion at that time was a much less popular idea among Western strategists, and it can be argued that it would not have been politically sustainable in Western-style democracies. Certainly, a policy by which the United States forces other countries into compliance (even its former superpower competitor, the Soviet Union) through the threat of a nuclear attack would neither have been conducive to strategic stability, nor would it have been a good fit for an internation-

---

[47] Echevarria, *Toward an American Way of War*, 2.

al order the United States was trying to build following the Second World War. This international order was based on international law, human rights, equality of nations, and an international economic system that allowed any state to succeed or fail based on individual national effort. Since the early years of the Cold War, deterrence—either conventional or nuclear—has taken up a central position in Western defense policy. Coercion occupies a second-rung position and is often seen as a last resort, if at all, when other nonkinetic options have failed.

From the Western perspective, then, the primary political use of the military is to either defeat the enemy adversary (a military objective that supports a political one) or to deter aggression. Philosophically, the West has problems justifying that an important purpose for the use of force by a country is to coerce other countries into compliance, or at least to do so and remain consistent with the Western theory of just war. Examples where the United States has used force coercively (e.g., Operations Enduring Freedom and Iraqi Freedom) have taken place under conditions in which the United States has been attacked first, or in which the target country was perceived to pose an extraordinary threat to the national security of the country.

Returning to the Chinese concept of power and its uses, the Chinese have no similar scruples about the purpose of the military. If it can be argued that Clausewitz served as the philosophical underpinning for how the West thinks about strategy and the military, we must now turn to Sun Tzu to obtain a corresponding Eastern view. Scholars of Sun Tzu observe that he made a similar statement to that of Clausewitz regarding the purpose of military.[48] In contrast to Clausewitz, Sun Tzu never claimed that the purpose of the military is to annihilate the ad-

---

[48] Michael Handel, *Sun Tzu and Clausewitz:* The Art of War *and* On War *Compared* (Carlisle, PA: U.S. Army War College Press, 1991).

versary's military for the purpose of imposing one's will on the other side.[49] Sun Tzu argued that the military is part of a more comprehensive policy of security that ultimately serves the political objective of the state. "The acme of skill," Sun Tzu writes in *The Art of War*, "is not for the General to win one hundred victories in one hundred battles." He continues, "To subdue the enemy without fighting is the acme of skill."[50] This can be accomplished through the skillful combination of a comprehensive strategy: a mix of diplomacy, economic statecraft, alliance formation, and the use of the military instrument. If the military can best aid in this endeavor by maneuvering itself into a position to then threaten something that the king of an adversary state loves (e.g., a city or a specific territory), then the general has made proper use of the military instrument.[51] If in doing so the strategist uses the military instrument to coerce the adversary into taking a course of action in line with one's own strategic objectives, then the strategist has done well.

Culturally, the Chinese have a much wider acceptance of the different uses of the military. The military can be built up to the extent that its *wei* (awesomeness) deters potential adversaries from attacking or coercing China (e.g., counterdeterrence against the United States). The military can be used to attack adversaries on China's periphery for the purposes of coaxing (or coercing) them into acceptance of Chinese dominance and punishing them for acting independent of Chinese interests (e.g., the Vietnam border clash of 1979). The military can seize territory of an adversary for the purposes of forcing them to negotiate a larger treaty defining the peace between China and the nation involved (e.g., the Sino-Indian border clash of 1962). The military can be used to bully, harass, and

---

[49] Sun Tzu, *The Art of War*, trans. Samuel Griffith (Oxford, UK: Oxford University Press, 1963), 77.

[50] Sun Tzu, *The Art of War*, 77.

[51] Sun Tzu, *The Art of War*, 77.

wear down smaller countries to force them into accepting Chinese negotiated terms for maritime territorial disputes (e.g., the South China Sea territorial disputes from the mid-1970s to the present). Finally, the military can ultimately be used to annihilate the army of the adversary so that the state can impose its will on the enemy—for example, the PLA during the Chinese Civil War. This discussion, as with the previous sections of this chapter, again illuminates an element of the strategic culture debate. In this case, the unique Chinese view of deterrence and coercion is supportive of the definition presented in the opening chapter of this book, in that a strategic culture is a distinctive body of beliefs, attitudes, and practices regarding the use of force, which are held by a collective and arise gradually over time through a unique, protracted historical process.

Stratagem: A Chinese Way of War?

As many scholars have described, Americans indeed have a peculiar way of war that contrasts distinctly with the way the Chinese have pursued war during their multimillennia history. To start with an American point of reference, historian Russell F. Weigley, in his well-known book on the American way of war, describes American warfighting throughout U.S. history as a combination of strategies focusing on attrition and wearing down one's opponents through battle.[52] This emphasis, Weigley noted, led to ever-increasing lethality and firepower to resolve military problems, and the ability to arrive at ingenious engineering and technological solutions.[53] This observation might even be extended to a Western way of war, championed by such scholars as Victor Davis Hanson, in which the history of militaries in the West are characterized by the arrival of new

---

[52] Russell F. Weigley, *The American Way of War: A History of United States Military Strategy and Policy* (Bloomington: Indiana University Press, 1960).
[53] Weigley, *The American Way of War*. Gen Ulysses S. Grant's campaigns during the latter part of the Civil War immediately come to mind.

technologies, a mastery of logistics, and a period of adaptation. As a result, strategists and military officers learn to apply new technologies to military problems and develop new military doctrine, and then strategists and heads of state apply the new military capabilities to strategy.[54] The history of warfare in the Western world can be described as a dynamic pattern dominated either by offensive weapons technology or defensive weapons technology.[55]

Arthur Waldron, the aforementioned scholar, notes that Chinese strategy and military endeavors, in contrast, have neither emphasized lethality and firepower nor engineering solutions. Moreover, he notes that Chinese military history is filled with examples where the contestants outmaneuvered forces, outwitted opponents, forced negotiations on their adversaries, or forced an adversaries' allies to switch sides, which dramatically changed the strategic situation. China has had its share of technological breakthroughs, and certainly the arrival of new technologies did have an effect on the battlefield and dictated outcomes. It is telling that China invented gunpowder in the ninth century CE, yet this new technological invention was not harnessed against China's Mongol enemies at the time—ironically, the Mongols overthrew the Chinese dynasty only one century thereafter.[56] Ultimately, the Chinese prefer maneuver over attrition to bring about a negotiated settlement instead of annihilation of the enemy through the introduction of some new weapon or technology.[57]

As opposed to the West, the most famous Chinese stories involving the military and warfare, Waldron notes, always

---

[54] Victor Davis Hanson, *Carnage and Culture: Battles in the Rise to Western Power* (New York: Random House, 2002).
[55] William H. McNeill, *The Pursuit of Power: Technology, Armed Force and Society Since A.D. 1000* (Chicago, IL: University of Chicago Press, 1984).
[56] Fairbank and Goldman, *China*, 115.
[57] Arthur Waldron, "China's Military Classics: A Book Essay," *Joint Force Quarterly*, no. 4 (Spring 1994): 114–17.

entailed stratagem and outwitting their opponent. The most famous such story, Luo Guanzhong's *Romance of the Three Kingdoms*, involves the hero, Zhuge Liang (181–234 CE), frequently outwitting his opponents on and off the battlefield. Even in the most famous foundational story in the West, Homer's *The Iliad*, in which the eventual outcome of the Trojan War is determined by stratagem and trickery, it needs to be recalled that the use of a Trojan horse still involved engineering a solution (the creation of the Trojan horse itself) and that the Greeks resorted to this stratagem after every other military option had been exhausted, including a direct assault on Troy. We can also see the differences between West and East in how the heroes are represented in these stories. In Chinese civilization the quintessential hero, Zhuge Liang, is most noted for his quick wit and ability to derive stratagems. In Homer's *The Iliad* and *The Odyssey*, although Odysseus ultimately comes up with the stratagem to defeat Troy (e.g., Trojan horse), the true hero is Achilles, famous for his attributes of strength and skill in killing his enemies on the battlefield. In the end, Western militaries to this day strategically or tactically depend on attrition, while the Chinese are interested in stratagem—including pressuring enemies to negotiate.[58]

Waldron observes that it is logical that Chinese civilization should prize stratagem and the ability to generate negotiated solutions to strategic problems. China encompassed territory far too vast, involving too large a population, and including too many powerful states or provinces for the central power to resolve all of its political problems through greater lethality. Chinese strategists had to come up with political-military solutions; they could not bully their way to controlling such a vast landmass and such a large population.[59] For most of its history,

---

[58] Waldron, "China's Military Classics."
[59] Waldron, "China's Military Classics," 114–17.

the Chinese central authorities had to govern an area of territory exceeding 1 million square miles.[60] Therefore, logistical, attrition-based warfare made little sense. As military professionals know, the overextension of lines of communication and supply lines leads to loss of power—not a position of strength.

A de-emphasis on technological change as the driver for strategy also makes sense from a geostrategic point of view. If one simply looks at a map of China, where would the Chinese state be confronted with relentless pressure from a peer competitor? China's geography makes China relatively isolated from Middle East rivals, particularly Iran and other major empires coming out of that region. Slavic empires did not emerge until much later along China's historical time lines. China dominated littoral Asia, with no threats coming from Japan, the Korean peninsula, or the Southeast Asian kingdoms. As mentioned before, the single most significant and persistent type of external threat to Chinese states were nomadic peoples, some of whom did develop military technologies—the mounted archer, the crossbow—to which China had to eventually confront and adapt. However, it was more often the case that Chinese statesmen ended up using political stratagems to neutralize threats. These stratagems included paying off invading tribes; forming alliances with one nomadic group of peoples against another; merging the children, especially the daughters of tribal chieftains, into noble Chinese families; and, if all else failed, absorbing a conquering nomadic enemy into Chinese culture itself (e.g., the Yuan and Qing dynasties were invading peoples who ended up becoming sinicized). In essence, Chinese heads of state and strategists are adept at formulating stratagems to manage a wide range of strategic problems; they are not prone to immediately go to an engineering solution or a strategy of attrition to solve security dilemmas.

---

[60] Waldron, "China's Military Classics," 114–17.

This preference for stratagem over engineering and technological solutions may explain, at least partially, how an advanced civilization such as China's could, in the nineteenth century, fall technologically behind compared to the West. Some Chinese historians have observed that the Chinese state was so large that its energies were focused on managing a large and significant bureaucracy; some historians blame Confucianism, with its emphasis on hierarchical relationships as leading to the dulling of the Chinese drive to innovate. Moreover, scholars of Chinese philosophy have pointed out that the philosophical worldview in China made it less inclined to the scientific method. That is, in Chinese philosophy and cosmology, the Chinese did not differentiate between a subjective world in which we live now and an objective "other" world where truth resides.[61] The Son of Heaven (*tianzi*) was sovereign of both the natural world and the supernatural world. In the West, by contrast, the American Judeo-Christian ethic is dominated by the idea of a monotheistic God who shall reveal universal truth at a time of their choosing. The Ancient Greeks also had a notion of a subjective world, and an objective world of truth as evidenced by Plato's story of the cave in which humans live in ignorance of universal truth, and it is the philosopher's calling to reveal truths to them through philosophical inquiry. These Western philosophical reference points contrast so deeply with Chinese thought that it is important to mark the points of departure.[62]

Interestingly, the single most significant technological surprise confronting the Chinese state was the arrival of the Western imperialist powers by the sea in the nineteenth century that

---

[61] Roger T. Ames, "The Confucian Worldview: Uncommon Assumptions, Common Misconceptions," in *Asian Texts, Asian Context: Encounters with Asian Philosophies and Religions*, ed. David Jones and E. R. Klein (Albany: State University of New York Press, 2010).

[62] Ames, "The Confucian Worldview."

forced the Chinese to reconsider its continentalist approach. The Chinese had no answer to superior seapower and a military capability marrying control of the sea with the ability to sustain expeditionary armies ashore for long periods of time. China's efforts to defeat this new type of threat through political stratagem proved fruitless. In the soul-searching that came out of the late nineteenth century to early- and mid-twentieth century humiliation of China, Chinese thinkers were convinced that mastering new technologies were central to meeting future threats to China, along with trying out new philosophies of governance—including Marxism-Leninism.

Consequently, it is the modern Chinese strategist's common historical and cultural experience that technology is vitally important, it needs to be developed indigenously, and if necessary it needs to be borrowed, bought, or stolen if only to ensure the survival of Chinese civilization. These technologies that are appropriated from the West must be carefully introduced into China, for today's Chinese, like their counterparts in the late nineteenth and early twentieth centuries, recognized that absorbing wholesale new technologies from foreign countries posed risks to the Chinese order. It is this balance of seeing the need to absorb advanced technology and new innovations while at the same time carefully screening the absorption of these new ideas that the Chinese frequently add the label "with Chinese characteristics" to imported foreign ideas or concepts to reflect this reality (e.g., "socialism with Chinese characteristics").

A strategic culture that stresses stratagem combined with a judicious pursuit of advanced technologies has manifested in interesting ways in China. First, the Chinese have spared no expense or effort to borrow, buy, or steal military technology from abroad.[63] The history of China's defense modernization is filled with this type of behavior. The Chengdu J-20 stealth fighter is essentially a platform entirely lifted from the American Lockheed Martin F-22 Raptor. The Chinese have learned how to mass produce surface combatants and arm them with longer ranges and more lethal surface-to-surface missiles. Additionally, they have for the past six years been experimenting with and learning how to operate off of an aircraft carrier acquired from Ukraine and have just recently introduced an indigenously produced carrier. The Chinese are said to soon produce a large deck amphibious ship, similar to a U.S. Navy landing helicopter dock (LHD). Notwithstanding the Chinese effort to pursue advanced technology through the concerted efforts of numerous special programs and offices, these efforts appear to be part of a larger Chinese strategy to gradually nudge the United States out of the Asia-Pacific; the pursuit of advanced technologies is conducted in conjunction with a number of coercive activities aimed at the countries of the region but designed to erode American credibility. Significantly, the American strategic response to China's defense modernization and its rise is to refocus efforts on widening the technology gap with China through a Third Offset Strategy and to enhance America's ability to operate in a heightened threat environment caused by Chinese technological advances through an Air-Sea Battle Concept.[64]

It is evident that China marries defense modernization and the incorporation of advanced technology with its military

---

[63] Phillip C. Saunders and Joshua K. Wiseman, "China's Quest for Advanced Aviation Technologies," in *The Chinese Air Force: Evolving Concepts, Roles, and Capabilities*, ed. Richard P. Hallion et al. (Washington, DC: National Defense University Press, 2012), 271–324.

[64] Mackenzie Eaglen, "What Is the Third Offset Strategy?," RealClearDefense, 15 February 2016; and Terry S. Morris et al. "Securing Operational Access: Evolving the Air-Sea Battle Concept," *National Interest*, 11 February 2015.

to accomplish political and strategic objectives through stratagem. If China's intention is to ultimately dominate the region and it intends to do so through a gradual erosion of American military effectiveness, then China's force-structure development will be designed to do just that. Through a steady and persistent development of Chinese military capabilities, coupled with the closing of the technology gap with the United States, the Chinese are sending a strong signal to the United States, its allies, and other countries of the region that they are here to stay, U.S. military technology superiority is waning, China will soon be in a position to keep the United States from intervening in the region, and the region will be left with a dominant Chinese military. The message China is sending is that it is better to align with China now before it is too late. Finally, this discussion on stratagem as representative of Chinese strategic culture highlights one of the definitions presented at the beginning of this book. That is, this case in particular defines strategic culture as a state or nonstate actor's shared beliefs and modes of behavior, derived from common experiences and narratives, which shapes the ends and means for achieving national security objectives.

Conclusion

This survey of Chinese strategic and cultural history illustrates that China's long and complicated history does not lend itself easily to broad generalizations about Chinese strategic behavior. In fact, China's extensive and lengthy experience with military and strategic issues provides opportunities for analysts on either side of a debate about China's future strategic trajectory to pick and choose what they want from history. At the same time, it must not be forgotten that the Chinese political leadership is unalterably marked by the fact that they live in a Leninist authoritarian system, and their most recent experience with war and conflict came about as a Communist polity. It cannot be denied that the Communist experience and the historical experiences associated with fighting the Chinese Civil War, the War of Resistance against Japan, the Korean conflict, and the Cold War had an indelible impact on Chinese strategic thinking. Beyond this observation, it is safe to say, however, that watching China's strategic behavior throughout its history has revealed a few patterns. First, the Chinese fervently believe that their strategic culture is defensive, even though Chinese history does not consistently support this view. The Chinese are not shy to use force if the use of force is designed to defend the state, or even to shape conditions enhancing the defense of the state. Second, the use of force within China has not always remained controlled and limited; sometimes the number of battlefield deaths in China's wars has numbered in the millions.

This tendency to see their actions as defensive, while being oblivious to the fact that others see their actions as aggressive, is illustrated by some of the actions recently undertaken by the Chinese in the South China Sea. Chinese island reclamation, militarizing the islets China controls in the area through the construction of airfields and ports, emplacing radar and surface-to-air missiles on these islets, harassing foreign fishermen, and increasing patrols in the area are but a few select examples of this dynamic.

There is also a geographic component to how the Chinese view strategy. For most of its history, China has had to worry more about security threats emanating from within the Asian continent, and not from the Asian littorals. This created a continentalist mind-set that had Chinese emperors fixated on the problem of managing threats from along China's steppes, which downplayed the significance of threats from the maritime domain. This strongly suggests that despite the Communist experience, the Chinese historical experience with its geography has made a significant impression on the Chinese perspective about how they think about security. Such a continentalist attitude only required changing when the British appeared from the sea and initiated a century and a half of humiliation for China. In adjusting to the shock of that threat coming from the sea, it can certainly be argued that the Chinese response, including the development of a modern navy and the pursuit of modern technology to ensure China's military would never be outgunned again by any foreign invader, reflects the beginning of a departure from a continentalist mentality.

While it is probably unlikely that China wants a formal tributary system requiring that modern vassal states pay homage to China, a good argument can be made that China does desire a hierarchical international relations structure in the Asia-Pacific. That hierarchy, of course, would involve China on the top with the other countries of the region below. China most likely aspires to dominate the region so convincingly that the leaders of the countries in the region dare not make decisions that would draw Beijing's ire. It goes without saying that, in this vision, the United States would have little influence or presence in the region.

One need only look at Chinese nuclear doctrine to conclude that China has a different perspective with regard to certain strategic concepts, such as deterrence. Its "no first use" declaratory doctrine as well as its reliance on a secure second strike with intercontinental ballistic missiles numbered only in the hundreds (as compared with the thousands of missiles possessed by the United States and Russia) suggest a strategic calculus quite different than that of either the United States or Russia during the Cold War. Additionally, China's employment of its conventional forces—part shows of force to elicit a deterrent effect, part coercive to prompt rivals to the negotiating table—strongly suggests that the Chinese have much wider latitude than many other countries on the state's use of the military as an instrument of policy.

Finally, Chinese force structure development and PLA

modernization appear to reflect a strategic outlook that combines both the pursuit of advanced technology (either through acquisitions from abroad or through indigenous efforts) with stratagems designed to generate substantial political effects favoring Chinese political objectives. Accordingly, we can conclude that the modernization efforts of the last two decades are designed to close the technological and capability gap between the two powers. The ultimate objective is to nudge the strategic environment toward a gradual departure of the United States from the region to a China dominating the region politically, economically, and militarily.

As stated at the beginning of this chapter, strategic culture cannot be used as a predictor of precise strategic and military decisions of a state. As Gray noted, there are too many factors going into a specific decision to be able to generalize that a certain historical event in a civilization's past is the exact cause of that decision. Strategic culture, however, can provide useful context in which we can understand the perception of decision makers as they review a variety of strategic options. Therefore, the fact that for most of China's history its leaders have had much more to worry about from continental threats than maritime ones does not preclude China from developing a blue water navy and a power projection capability; at the same time, a continentalist mind-set would help explain China's behavior over the past few decades. Why no full-fledged overseas military bases? Why the peculiar name of People's Liberation Army Navy? Why has China's military organization, until now, been structured on geographical internal defense and not on missions abroad, despite its increasing interests abroad? Strategic culture will not predict what China's leaders will choose on their menu of strategic options; however, it will help us to understand what their preferences have been in the past, and why, and those preferences could shape the choices they pick in the future.

CHAPTER
3

DOES AFGHANISTAN HAVE A "STRATEGIC CULTURE"?

by Vern Liebl

Pull out your swords and slay anyone that says Pashtun and Afghan are not one! Arabs know this and so do Romans; Afghans are Pashtuns, Pashtuns are Afghans![1]

In a recent publication, Ashley J. Tellis wrote, "All states arguably have unique strategic cultures, which invariably shape their political behaviors. The accumulation and use of national power, including material military capabilities, are constantly shaped by historical and social context."[2] This is a fairly clear-cut statement, yet one has to wonder if the author ever really looked at Afghanistan. However, the purpose of this chapter

---

[1] Pashtun warrior poet and scholar, chief of the Khattaks, who died in 1698. Extract from Khushal Khan Khattak, "Passion of the Afghan," in *Afghan Poetry of the 17th Century: Selections from the Poems of Khushal Khan Khattak*, trans. C. E. Biddulph (London: Kegan Paul, Trench, Trubner, 1890). Today, the Khattak tribe, with nearly 3 million members, spans the border of Pakistan and Afghanistan. They are part of the larger Kakai Karlanri confederacy.

[2] Ashley J. Tellis, "Understanding Strategic Cultures in the Asia-Pacific," in *Strategic Asia 2016–17: Understanding Strategic Cultures in the Asia-Pacific*, ed. Michael Wills et al. (Washington, DC: National Bureau of Asian Research).

is not to address the academic definition of strategic culture, as one can refer to Stuart Poore's 2003 article exploring the debate between Colin S. Gray and Alastair Iain Johnston.[3] This is more about how a people—in particular, those who we refer to as Afghans, and who are certainly not a homogeneous ethnic or linguistic grouping of people—view themselves through the nation-state context or through the strategic culture lens. Indeed, the Afghans do not consider themselves as a homogenous ethnic or linguistic group, but by taking this into account as we compare their experience with what we expect of nation-states, we can gain a better understanding of a country that has defied Western categorizations for most of its history, as Khushal Khan Khattak indicated above.[4]

Is Afghanistan a State?

Before exploring whether Afghanistan has a strategic culture—and if it does, what it may look like—there needs to be at least a brief exploration of whether Afghanistan can be considered a state, a nation, or possibly neither. Clearly, if the definition of *state* is explained as an entity that concerns all institutions and laws that organizes the public life of a group of people within a given territorial boundary (however elastic and temporary it may be in a political and historical sense), then it is a state in that meaning. Therefore, the next query concerns nationhood.

---

[3] Stuart Poore, "What Is the Context?: A Reply to the Gray-Johnston Debate on Strategic Culture," *Review of International Studies* 29, no. 2 (April 2003): 279–84, https://doi.org/10.1017/S0260210503002791.

[4] There have been some efforts to categorize Afghanistan; for three examples, see Shahmahmood Miakhel, "The Importance of Tribal Structures and Pakhtunwali in Afghanistan: Their Role in Security and Governance," in *Challenges and Dilemmas of State-building in Afghanistan: Report of a Study Trip to Kabul*, ed. Arpita Basu Roy (Delhi: Shipra Publications, 2008), 97–110; Jennifer Keister, "The Illusion of Chaos: Why Ungoverned Spaces Aren't Ungoverned, and Why that Matters," *Cato Institute Policy Analysis*, no. 766, 9 December 2014; and Elliott Averett, "Lines in the Sand: The Strategic Culture in the Afghan Taliban," *Midwest Journal of Undergraduate Research*, no. 6 (2016): 94–119.

Is Afghanistan a nation? Usually *nation* and *state* are used synonymously, as *nation-state* describing a single cohesive entity. In reality, the term *nation* can actually be described as something similar to an ethnic group that gives political meaning to their aggregate identity. Still, the very definition of the word nation does not actually clarify the situation. Nation, from the Latin *natio*—people, tribe, kin, genus, class, flock—is a social concept most commonly used to designate larger groups or collections of people with common characteristics attributed to them, including language, traditions, customs, habits, and ethnicity. With this definition, a community of people with a similar language, habits, and ethnicity can be a nation. In other words, Afghanistan clearly has several different nations—Pashtuns, Tajiks, Hazara, Uzbeks, and more. So, Afghanistan may be termed a *nation of nations*.

As a pragmatic principle, when examining Kosovo, China, and Brazil in the other chapters of this book, they tend to possess one national identity and one language despite ethnic diversity. However, in reality, there are exceptions, such as the ethnic divisions within the same linguistic grouping like the Serbo-Croats, as a contrarian example. Unlike in some other countries with significant minorities or increasing numbers of immigrants, the overwhelming majority of the people in the three named countries are ethnically and/or culturally alike with a reasonably uniform cultural narrative. It is therefore relatively easy to examine what is or may be the strategic culture of such states.

Ethnicity and Identity as Factors

Afghanistan, despite Western presumptions, is not dominated by one ethnic group.[5] In fact, just looking at the current

---

[5] For a recent exploration of this topic, see Whitney Azoy, "Post-Buffer Afghanistan: A Nation-State Here to Stay?," in *Afghanistan, 1979–2009: In the Grip of Conflict* (Washington, DC: Middle East Institute, 2009), 14–16.

Afghan national anthem is quite illustrative as to the ethnic complexities of Afghanistan:

This land is Afghanistan—It is the pride of every Afghan
The land of peace, the land of the sword—Its sons are all brave
This is the country of every tribe—Land of Baluch, and Uzbeks
Pashtoons, and Hazaras—Turkman and Tajiks with them,
Arabs and Gojars, Pamirian, Nooristanis
Barahawi, and Qizilbash—Also Aimaq, and Pashaye
This Land will shine for ever—Like the sun in the blue sky
In the chest of Asia—It will remain as the heart for ever
We will follow the one God
We all say, Allah is great, we all say, Allah is great[6]

And they all claim to be Afghans. So it can be described as a nation, even if the 14 ethnicities identified in the national anthem, and the other even smaller groups not mentioned, maintain their own specific cultural narratives. This suggests that some form of strategic culture exists in that it remains one state despite its multitude of identities and 38 years of conflict. The nearly four decades of fighting began in December 1979 when the Soviets invaded Afghanistan. The 10-year-long Soviet intervention (it clearly was not an occupation as Soviet troops did not physically occupy most of the country but did devastate large portions by air attacks) ended in 1989. It gave way to the Warlord Era (1989–96), followed by the Afghan Civil War/Taliban era (1996–2001), and then the U.S. intervention/Kabul government period (2001–present).

---

[6] Adopted in 2006, the anthem is called the "Surud-e Milli" in Dari and "Milli Surood" in Pashto.

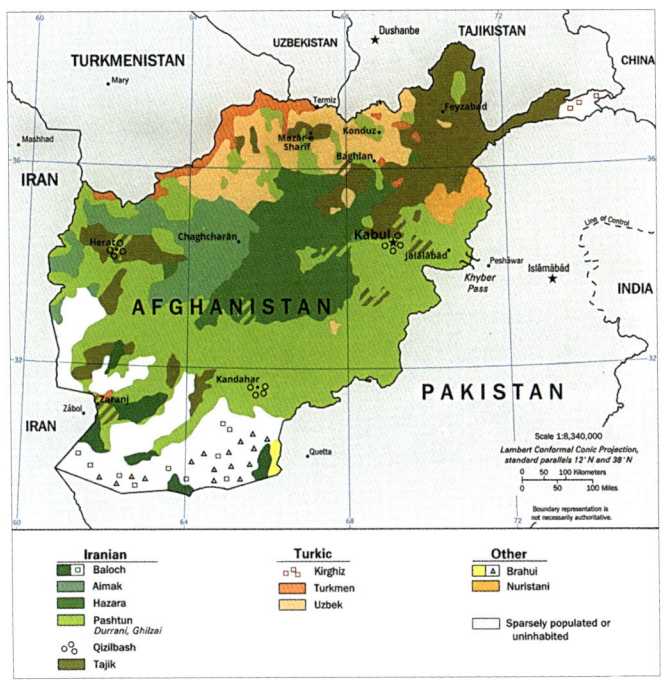

MAP 1

U.S. Central Intelligence Agency, adapted by MCU Press

Despite possessing numerous potential catalysts for division and secession, there has been no major separatist movement to remove one or more ethnic groups from Afghanistan to join with any of the surrounding states, namely Iran, Pakistan, Tajikistan, Uzbekistan, and Turkmenistan (map 1).[7]

---

[7] In 2004, the author was told a story while in Afghanistan that, when Afghans were polled in late 2003 about the future of Afghanistan, not one of the 300 responses advocated breaking it up by ethnicity or language. There is no "reliable source" for this information, but it was frequently repeated within the Combined Joint Task Force 180 headquarters in Bagram as well as in the subsequent Combined Forces Command-Afghanistan headquarters, specifically among civil affairs and intelligence personnel.

Unhelpful as Neighbors

Two groups provide some support to separatist movements in other countries, one comprised of a small number of Pamiris in Badakhshan (mainly in the Wakhan Corridor area), who support the majority Pamiris of Gorno-Badakhshan autonomous oblast, a mountainous region in eastern Tajikistan.[8] The other ethnic group are the Baloch of southern Afghanistan, some of whom support their ethnic relatives in Pakistan and Iran in their conflict with those respective governments.[9] In the 1930s, there was an expatriate group of Turkmen and Uzbeks who supported the Basmachi Revolt in Central Asia against the Soviets, but that essentially died out due to thorough defeat in Central Asia, with most of the expatriates moving on to Turkey in the 1940s and 1950s. In none of the above instances was there any effort to divide Afghanistan; rather, their goals tended to involve attempts to fragment neighboring countries.

However, there are the Pashtuns, the largest ethnic group within Afghanistan (see map 1), some of whom could be described as irredentists. This means that they would like to see portions of modern Pakistan inhabited by Pashtuns restored to Afghanistan. There are some problems with this.

The Pashtuns of Afghanistan supposedly number around 13 million, although the last census was conducted in 1979 when a total of 15.5 million inhabitants of all ethnicities were counted. Today, the number of inhabitants in Afghanistan is

---

[8] The majority of Pamiris in the Gorno-Badakhshan autonomous oblast are Ismaili Muslims (or Nizari Sevener Shia) and are being supported in their very low-level insurgency by the Aga Khan Foundation, a charity not known for links to any insurgencies.

[9] In Iran, this support is often given to Jaish al-Adl (or Army of Justice) and/or Harakat Ansar Iran (or Partisan Movement of Iran). In Pakistan, this Afghan Baloch support is given to multiple organizations; the Baloch National Front (a political umbrella organization) and/or the Baloch Liberation Army (BLA), based both in Afghanistan and Pakistan. Interestingly, Pakistan and the United Kingdom have declared the BLA a terrorist organization, but the European Union, India, and the United States have not declared it as such.

estimated at between 29 and 36 million, which allows for the increase in Afghan Pashtuns. Or, if one estimates the proportion of Pashtuns at approximately 42 percent, extrapolating from the 1979 census and applying that to 2017 population figures, that gives the current estimate of 13 million Pashtuns.[10] The irredentist theme results from the many Afghan Pashtuns who would like to reincorporate their Pakistani Pashtun brethren into Afghanistan. Pashtuns in Pakistan comprise almost 16 percent of the population, or approximately 31 million Pashtuns.[11] To date, there has been no groundswell of support among Pashtuns in Pakistan for joining with their Afghan brethren to form "Pashtunistan"—an old concept that includes vast areas where Pashtuns have not historically lived, such as all of Balochistan, much of the Hazarajat, and extensive Tajik-inhabited areas. Basically, this is an advocacy by Afghan Pashtuns to enlarge Afghanistan at the expense of Pakistan.

The Near-Abroad Pashtuns[12]

Some "Pakistani Pashtuns" provide support to Afghanistan-based insurgent groups, such as the Taliban, and some Pakistan-based Pashtun tribes are trying to supplant Afghanistan-based Pashtun (or Baloch) tribes by physically displacing them. The primary example would be the Kakar tribe of the Gurghusht tribal confederation. The Gurghusht, who occupy Pakistan's western border region of the Balochistan Province, have worked to physically and violently replace the Alikozai tribe of the Durrani tribal confederation, out of Sangin District in

---

[10] Although, the *2015 CIA World Factbook* holds the Afghanistan Pashtun population at 10.75 million.

[11] This number comes from the *2012 CIA World Factbook*; accurately counting Pashtuns in either country is difficult at best.

[12] Pashtuns living in Pakistan refer to themselves as Afghans. It is the rare Pashtun who identifies as a Pakistani, which for almost all Pashtuns indicates a *Punjabi*, which is an insulting term.

Afghanistan's Helmand Province.[13] This entire effort is camouflaged by the Taliban conflict in southern Afghanistan, abetted by the struggle to control the opium trafficking network. However, the Kakar-Alikozai struggle cannot be classified as an irredentist movement or a separatist movement, as it is an intraethnic or intranational tribal war.

If the surrounding neighbors of Afghanistan are examined (even including the Pashtun tribes in Pakistan), one would find little, if any, evidence of irredentist desire to divide Afghanistan by either ethnic division or absorption of "kindred" ethnicities. Pakistan loudly declaims it wants no territory or peoples of Afghanistan.[14] Apparently the thought of more Pashtuns is unpalatable at best, and Pakistan wants to formalize the Durand Line as a permanent border versus a frontier.[15] For the peoples of western India, the Pashtuns represented the diabolical "other" and were the nightmares of many Hindu and Sikh Punjabi children for centuries—on the Hindu Kush mountains of Afghanistan, the name is believed to be Persian for "killer of Hindus."

The people of Iran do not want to recover any part of Afghanistan lost to the Pashtuns. Despite some cultural affinity with the Farsiwan (or Persian speakers) of western Afghanistan,

---

[13] The author discovered this while working in Afghanistan, as he was the officer in charge of the Joint Document Exploitation Cell. Numerous captured documents from southeastern Afghanistan indicated this intratribal conflict and the drive to dispossess the Alikozai out of Sangin (Sangeen) by the Kakar tribe.

[14] Anatol Lieven, "Afghanistan: What Pakistan Wants," *New York Review of Books*, 15 July 2013.

[15] The Durand Line is the 2,640-kilometer (1,640-mile) border between Afghanistan and Pakistan created by an agreement between Sir Mortimer Durand, secretary of the British Indian government, and Abdur Rahman Khan, the emir of Afghanistan, which was signed on 12 November 1893. It has served as the official border between the two nations for more than 100 years, but has been the source of much controversy because, when the Durand Line was created, Pakistan was still a part of India, which was controlled by the United Kingdom from 1858 until India's independence in 1947. Pakistan also became a nation in 1947.

Iran has no desire to fight over Herat, as it has been ruled largely by Pashtuns since the early 1700s. Linguistically linked to both the Aimaq, the Tajiks, and even the Hazara, the Persians are ethnically distinct from all three groups.[16] Even the near-war of 1998 between the Islamic Emirate of Afghanistan and Iran was provoked by the Taliban murder of Iranian diplomatic personnel, not over issues of land or ethnic irredentism.

Afghanistan's northern neighbors—Turkmenistan, Uzbekistan, and Tajikistan—have no designs or desires for any Afghan territory. Those ethnic minorities in Afghanistan show no interest at all in seceding from Afghanistan and joining with those countries. For example, Uzbekistan has shown a willingness to host, in small numbers over the past few decades, Afghan Uzbek refugees, but they also have displayed an equal willingness to encourage the return of those refugees back to Afghanistan as soon as possible.[17] Most of the Uzbek in Afghanistan are descended from refugees who fled Soviet forces in the 1920s and 1930s, having drifted apart from the remaining Uzbeks who survived the ministrations of Sovietization. All three named countries are far more concerned with their own internal security, meaning insurgent and separatist groups, than with Afghanistan.[18]

In sum, to all five of the above countries, there are no irredentist claims on Afghanistan and there are no ethnic rebellions to be fomented, the Kakar tribal invasion notwith-

---

[16] All three ethnic groups speak closely related varieties of modern Persian, which is Farsi. The Tajiks of Afghanistan number approximately 11 million, the Hazara number approximately 6 million, and the Aimaq number approximately 1 million. The Persians of Iran openly discriminate against all three groups if they reside in Iran, especially the Hazara and the Aimaq, who often look Mongolic.

[17] Gabriel Dominguez, "Why Central Asia Is Increasingly Worried about Afghanistan," DW, 4 November 2015.

[18] For a good examination of the relations between Afghanistan and the Central Asian republics, see Christian Bleuer and S. Reza Kazemi, *Between Co-operation and Insulation: Afghanistan's Relations with the Central Asian Republics* (Kabul, Afghanistan: Afghanistan Analysts Networks, 2014).

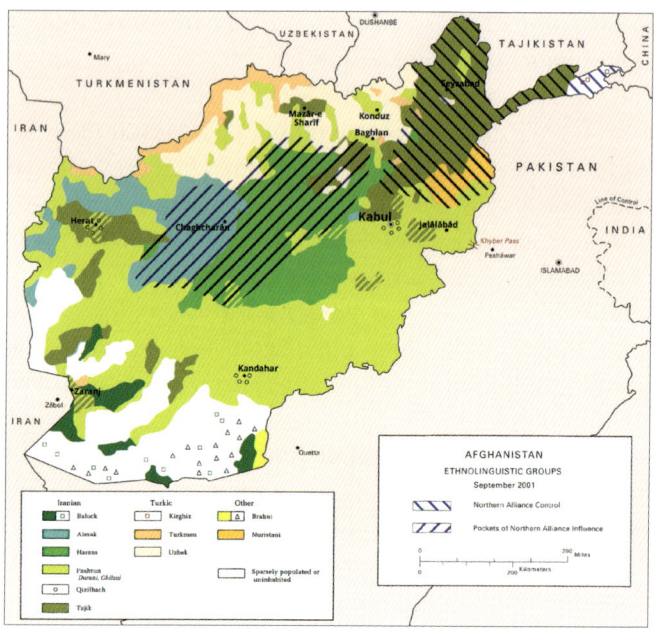

MAP 2
U.S. Army, adapted by MCU Press

standing. Additionally, none of the surrounding countries see any economic or strategic payoff even if they had designs to invade, occupy, or partition Afghanistan (map 2).

Looking at Afghanistan, there is opportunity for division, or to find support to weaken or divide the country into fragments. Pakistan is not at all shy in trying to manipulate Pashtun tribal factions to target an ethnicity or even incite sectarian strife in an effort to keep Afghanistan weak and divided. Pakistan uses these techniques to mitigate the historical threat of Afghan invasion and incursion eastward across the Indus River. Pakistan is trying to manage what it sees as not a military threat but more of a tribal (divisiveness) and social stability (criminality) security issue, and it is also engaged in a proxy conflict against India within Afghanistan. India supports Afghanistan precisely as a counterweight to Pakistan, diplomatically and economically where possible, and covertly via intelligence and support to anti-Pakistani insurgent organizations (e.g., the Baloch Liberation Army or BLA).

Yet, Afghanistan, as a case study for strategic culture, does provide insight into the concept and how to apply it to a place or places that seem unlikely to have strategic culture. By looking at Afghanistan's history, there are historical and cultural patterns that can aid military advisors, analysts, and civilian scholars to better understand those places that do not seem to fit the definitive categories of strategic culture.

Afghanistan's Historical and Cultural Context

The region that is now Afghanistan has been a part of the history of kingdoms and empires, very often divided among several. Due to its location, it has often been a crossroads as well, seeing conquering or defeated foreign armies usually moving east or west, usually committing widespread depredations in passing. But by the middle of the seventeenth century, something was achieved that marked the beginning of what we might call the modern world system, leading inadvertently to conditions that would help create an identifiable state of Afghanistan. This would also allow for an unexpected and disproportionate role for Afghans on the world stage.

Mercantile-based Imperial Era

This modern world system of the mid-seventeenth century was marked specifically by the creation of economic networks. The Dutch Republic (Republic of the United Netherlands), headquartered out of Amsterdam and building on the earlier efforts of the Spanish and Portuguese, managed to incorporate local and regional trade linkages into what history has come to recognize as the first global hegemonic power of the "capitalist" world economy.[19] This was a prodigious and rare feat in world history subsequently achieved later only by Great Britain and the United States.[20] The Dutch traded through a series of corporations, via outposts and factories in such places as Recife, Brazil, in New Amsterdam (which became New York), and dozens of other locations. The largest corporation was the Verenigde Oost-Indische Compagnie, or the Dutch East Indies Company, normally identified as the VOC.[21] The VOC controlled the most profitable portion of this new global economic entity, and a huge portion of that profit came out of trade with the Safavid Empire in Persia, which traded for, or more usually bought European goods, paying in silver.[22] The Safavid Empire forces occupied as colonial territory most of what today would be referred to as southern and eastern Afghanistan, an area populated by Pashtuns.

In 1721, the Hotaki Pashtuns in that Safavid-ruled region rose in rebellion. By 1722, the Hotakis had not only freed themselves but had essentially driven the Safavid Empire out of existence except for some dynastic fragments who never re-

[19] It was neither truly a free market à la Adam Smith nor was it truly mercantilist, but it demonstrated characteristics that presaged modern capitalism.

[20] Jeffrey R. Macris and Saul Kelly, eds., *Imperial Crossroads: The Great Powers and the Persian Gulf* (Annapolis: Naval Institute Press, 2012), 16.

[21] A factory, from the Latin "to do," was an establishment for factors (Latin—"doer") engaged in the selling and receiving of goods on commission, usually transacting business without disclosing their principal. Typically located for safety and access, these could be called trading posts and were, in South Asia, often precursors to colonial expansion. In South Asia, the initial factories were established by the Portuguese (*feitoria*) in the fifteenth century, ultimately being displaced by the Dutch (*factorij*), the French (*factorerie*), and mostly by the English, except around Goa. Factories served simultaneously as market, warehouse, customs post, defense, support to navigation or exploration, and as the de facto headquarters or government of local communities. For more, see James D. Tracy, ed., *The Political Economy of Merchant Empires: State Power and World Trade, 1350–1750* (Cambridge, UK: Cambridge University Press, 1997), https://doi.org/10.1017/CBO9780511665288.

[22] Macris and Kelly, *Imperial Crossroads*, 17–18.

gained significant power or stature before being swept from history a few years later. This explosion of "Afghans" from the region of Kandahar, completely unforeseen, destroyed the economy of Safavid Persia, which immediately stopped trade with the VOC. The unforeseen loss of silver income sent a severe shock through the company. By 1725, the VOC was forced to retrench its economic and political networks, withdrawing from the Persian Gulf. It reconsolidated in a much-reduced structure in what would become known as the Dutch Nederlands Oost-Indie, or the Netherlands East Indies, basically ceding the western Indian Ocean to a new and upcoming trading power, the British joint-stock East India Company (or EIC).

By the early 1760s, the EIC was making astounding economic and political inroads into the Indian subcontinent territory. The EIC was freed from any serious competition from the Dutch, and the EIC was not seriously hindered by the French in the Indian Ocean during the global Seven Years' War of 1756–63. The major limiting factors for the EIC at this time were the Moghul Empire, a declining but still powerful entity, as well as the rising Maratha Empire.

Yet, the impact of Afghans again changed everything. The Hotaki Afghans had been defeated by the Persian Afsharid Empire in 1738. The Afshari, with the death of Nader Shah in 1747, were then subsumed by a new Pashtun "explosion," this time called the Abdali, who renamed themselves the Durrani.[23] By 1750, Persia was conquered by the Durrani, who then repeatedly invaded India. By 1767, the Durrani forces had essentially destroyed the declining Moghul Empire, whose rem-

---

[23] The 1747 Pashtun revolt against Nader Shah was led by an Abdali tribal leader, who was the captain of Nader Shah's bodyguard, Abdul Khan. He assumed power as the emir of the Abdali, which he achieved by stealing the now dead Nader Shah's mobile treasury and spreading it among the other Abdali tribal leaders. He then changed his name to Padshah durr-I durran, meaning "King, pearl of the age." The Abdali tribal confederacy was thus renamed the Durrani.

nants would later be completely swept away by Britain in the wake of the 1857 Sepoy Mutiny. The rising Maratha Empire was brutally cudgeled into impotence with its remnants to be protected by the British Raj after 1818, for British economic and imperial benefit.[24] These Durrani-led Afghan invasions and extensive destruction gave the EIC, and also the rising British imperial forces, a much stronger hand to act against greatly weakened regional powers throughout South Asia and ultimately drove others, such as the Sikhs, Rajputs, Punjabis, Baloch, and Sindhis, into the arms of the British as imperial volunteers or as allied princely state military forces.

The Durrani Afghans, through a series of vicious and self-destructive dynastic succession struggles, greatly weakened the western geographic part of the Indian subcontinent, allowing for extensive EIC and British imperial penetration. This British expansion also attracted imperial Russian interest vis-à-vis British interests in Afghanistan, especially security from Pashtun invasion or raiding and as an imperial buffer zone, as well as resurgent Persian Qajar interest in the Herat region.[25] By the early 1800s, the area today called Afghanistan was vital to the British as an area that no one else controlled to better secure the British Raj of the Indian subcontinent.

---

[24] The Marathas were a Hindu warrior group originally from the Deccan Plateau, who in the mid-seventeenth century revolted from the Muslim Mughal Empire. They managed to establish a Hindavi Swarajya (an area of Hindu self-governance) in former Mughal lands. It was the Mughal-Maratha Wars of 1680–1707 that, in conjunction with the religious excesses of Mughal emperor Aurengzeb (ruled 1659–1707), was the main cause for the decline of the Mughals. The Durrani victory in 1761 over the Marathas at the Third Battle of Panipat (approximately 95,000 Maratha dead) checked forever Maratha expansion.

[25] The Qajars were a Persian dynasty of Turkic origin who reclaimed eastern Persia from the Durrani Afghans and united it with western Persian (being ruled by the Lurish Zand dynasty from 1751–96). They ruled Persia from 1789 to 1925. It was the Qajars who provoked the Anglo-Persian War of 1856 over Herat, the British preventing Qajar repossession of Herat and making it a permanent part of Afghanistan. For more, see Abbas Amanat, *The Pivot of the Universe: Nasir al-Din Shah and the Iranian Monarchy, 1831–1896*, rev. ed. (London: I. B. Tauris, 2008).

Imperial Competition

This series of events initiated what became known as the "Great Game."[26] It can best be described as an imperial geopolitical contest primarily between Britain and Russia, but with other minor players, such as the previously mentioned Qajar and on occasion the French, Ottomans, and Chinese. Afghanistan was the main locus of this long rivalry, initiated by competition in Central Asia bringing expansion of the Russian Empire and the concomitant destruction of the Khiva and Bukhara Emirates by the Russians. This Russian expansion and British failure to succor the emirates brought the Russians to the inchoate frontiers of the British protectorate of Afghanistan. This presence, along with Russian diplomatic ventures into British India and suggested hints at support of the Afghan emir, induced Britain to adopt a forward defense posture in Afghanistan. Subsequent British and Russian machinations in the Persian Gulf, involving the Persian Qajars over the issue of Herat, ultimately led to further British intrusion into the littoral areas of the Persian Gulf. Likewise, Russian, French, and Ottoman competition in Jerusalem provided flammable tender for the Crimean War of 1853–56 in the distant Black Sea, where Britain felt obligated to aid the Ottomans and French specifically because of the Russian-British rivalry over Afghanistan. Completely

---

[26] The *Great Game* is a term historians use to refer to a period of conflict and maneuver throughout Central Asia, the Caucasus, and Afghanistan beginning in 1930 and not ending until the 1920s. The primary players were Great Britain and Russia. For more, see Martin Ewans et al., *The Great Game: Britain and Russia in Central Asia,* vol. 1, *Documents* (London: Routledge Curzon, 2004); Martin Ewans, *Securing the Indian Frontier in Central Asia: Confrontation and Negotiation, 1865–1895* (London: Routledge Curzon, 2010); *The Imperial Gazetteer of India: The Indian Empire,* vol. IV, *Administrative* (Oxford: Clarendon Press, 1908), xxx, 552; Sneh Mahajan, *British Foreign Policy, 1874–1914: The Role of India* (London: Routledge, 2001); Gerald Morgan, "Myth and Reality in the Great Game," *Asian Affairs* 4, no. 1 (1973): 55–65, https://doi.org/10.1080/03068377308729652; and Gerald Morgan, *Anglo-Russian Rivalry in Central Asia: 1810–1895* (London: Routledge, 1981).

aside from the political machinations, and from a personal level, Afghanistan was accepted by Britain as the place where an Englishman could prove his manhood in the Victorian era of Rudyard Kipling.[27] Afghanistan became a locus of romantic danger, not a "state" feared as an invader.

Following the First World War, Afghanistan temporarily slipped from the global stage, although Turkish efforts to create a regional ally provided a stabilizing influence to the kingdom as it roiled with Soviet jockeying along its northern frontier (the previously mentioned Basmachi Revolt, the flight of refugee Uzbeks into Afghanistan, and the occasional Soviet "hot pursuit") and several internal Pashtun rebellions (antimodernization uprisings). The era of imperial powers jockeying for control over present-day Afghanistan ended in the early 1920s, when the newly ascendant Soviets drove the British (and French) from the Caucasus, of which one side effect was to finally delineate the northern borders of the kingdom of Afghanistan.[28]

In Afghanistan, a Tajik briefly supplanted the Barakzai Durrani Pashtuns in 1929, but Pashtun political dominance

[27] Rudyard Kipling's poem "Arithmetic on the Frontier" is a good literary example of this. That it was fully reciprocated by Pashtuns can best be seen in T. L. Pennell, *Among the Wild Tribes of the Afghan Frontier: A Record of Sixteen Years' Close Intercourse with the Natives of the Indian Marches* (London: Seeley, 1909).

[28] Afghanistan invaded British India in May 1919, quickly being repelled by a depleted Indian Army, primarily via the use of British airpower. This is known as the Third Anglo-Afghan War. Stalemated, Afghanistan and Britain signed the Treaty of Rawalpindi in 1919, which recognized the independence of the Emirate of Afghanistan and removed British subsidies. In 1926, the emir, Amanullah Khan, declared himself king and Afghanistan a kingdom. Additionally, Afghanistan and the Soviet Union had a minor military clash over the island of Urta-Tugai in the Amu Darya. It was initially occupied by Soviet troops; Afghan forces attacked them and ultimately a treaty was signed that specifically delineated the northern frontier. See Sergei Borisovich Panin, "Soviet-Afghan Conflict of 1925–26 over the Island of Urta-Tugai," *Journal of Slavic Military Studies* 12, no. 3 (1999): 122–33, https://doi.org/10.1080/13518049908430405.

was quickly reimposed.[29] As the Second World War neared, Japanese and German engineers began the long effort to tame the Helmand River, an ongoing effort today. The Afghan government, led by King Mohammad Zahir Shah, while favoring the Axis, remained one of the few countries in the world that managed to sit out the war. Despite being neutral during the Second World War, Afghanistan was rife with foreign agents, primarily Italian for the Axis and British for the Allies, and occasionally prominent in Axis plans aimed at disrupting the British in India or, less often, aimed at disrupting the Allied position in Persia.

Soviet Intervention and Aftermath

Post–Second World War Afghanistan under King Zahir Shah began an intensive program aimed at modernizing the country, an effort that grew increasingly unpopular among much of the populace. The king's prime minister, Muhammad Daoud Khan, who was also his cousin, became the prime motivating agent behind the modernization efforts. It was Daoud who requested assistance from both the United States and the Soviet Union, beginning a foreign aid race over Afghanistan by both powers. Daoud overthrew his cousin, the king, in 1973, dissatisfied with the slow pace of modernization the king wanted and invited greater Soviet influence in Afghanistan. It was the

---

[29] Habibullah Kalakani, an ethnic Persian from a small village north of Kabul. In 1929, with the Afghan Army distracted by Pashtun discontent in Nangarhar and Laghman provinces, Kalakani led a minor antimodernization revolt and attacked Kabul from the north. Aided by a serendipitous attack against southern Kabul by Waziri tribesmen from Paktia, he pressured the king into abdicating to him. Assuming the kingship in January 1929, he ruled for nine months, working to erase all traces of modernization, sometimes brutally. He was overthrown by Muhammad Nadir Shah, who reasserted the Barakzai dynastic line. Hanged two weeks after being deposed, he was buried in an unmarked grave. In September 2016, his reburial by the Ghani administration became political, ultimately resulting in one death and four injured. The Pashtuns refer to him by his pejorative nickname, which is Bacha-i-Saqao, or "water carrier's son."

increased influence of the Soviets in the 1960s and 1970s, the Saur Revolution in 1978, and then a regime change in 1979 that led to Soviet assistance to Afghanistan with the intervention of the Soviet *40th Combined Arms Army*.

Lasting almost a decade, the Soviet occupation of Afghanistan, later called the Limited Contingent of Soviet Force-Afghanistan (LCSF-A), witnessed the deaths of approximately 2 million Afghans as well as forcing approximately 7 million into refugee status (with more than 4 million flooding into Pakistan).[30] The Soviets lost 14,500 military personnel and 55,000 wounded before withdrawing. As imperial wars go historically, this was not a conflict that would seem to have been an existential threat to the Soviet Union, but it was. The Union of Soviet Socialist Republics (USSR) was vastly overcommitted globally, with more than 5.5 million servicemembers under arms.[31] The Soviets had to deploy multiple military components, such as ground forces, navy, air force, Air Defense Forces, Strategic Rocket Forces, KGB (Komitet Gosudarstvennoy Bezopasnosti or "Committee for State Security") military units, and Ministry of Internal Affairs internal police forces—many deployed in Europe as part of Warsaw Pact forces or along the Chinese border in the Far East. While the approximately 115,000 soldiers of the LCSF-A do not appear to be a large draw on Soviet manpower requirements, this was the first significant loss suffered by the Soviet Union, one inflicted by lightly armed religious guerrillas. That this was combined with casualty numbers made the losses a critical fact worth noting at the time as well as in the present. Indeed, historians have referred to Afghanistan as the Soviet's equivalent to the American intervention in Vietnam; invasion and occupation drained the Soviet economy and

[30] Marek Sliwinski, "Afghanistan: The Decimation of a People," *Orbis* 33, no. 1 (Winter 1989): 9.

[31] Steven W. Popper, *The Economic Cost of Soviet Military Manpower Requirements* (Santa Monica, CA: Rand, 1989).

has been cited as an internal weakness leading to the fall of the USSR.[32] The Soviet withdrawal from Afghanistan, portrayed as voluntary in 1989, was followed by the rejection of the USSR's rule by Soviet Bloc nations. Between 1989 and 1990, nationalist movements in Poland, Hungary, East Germany, Czechoslovakia, Bulgaria, and Romania, and the refusal of the Soviet leadership to commit military force to crush those movements, led to the dissolution of the Soviet Union in July 1991.

Soviet involvement in Afghanistan was the last in a string of internal and external pressures that strained the Soviet Union and led to its collapse. That does not mean things suddenly became delightful for the people of Afghanistan. Withdrawal of a superpower also meant a loss of resources desperately needed to rebuild a completely devastated region, to reestablish a state structure, and to provide a safe future for Afghans of all ethnic groups. Pakistan extensively manipulated the internal situation of Afghanistan and exploited instability, ably funded by Islamist organizations from the Arabian Peninsula. Civil war exploded, adding further death and destruction. The dire situation created the conditions for the rise of a religious group, the Taliban, who by 1998 had assumed the status of a state called the Islamic Emirate of Afghanistan. It ultimately controlled almost 90 percent of Afghanistan by 2001.

At this juncture, Afghanistan again forcibly inserted itself onto the world stage. It was in Afghanistan that the terrorist organization al-Qaeda coordinated, funded, and selected the individuals who participated in the hijacked airliner attacks on U.S. targets on 11 September 2001. Initially stunned, the United States invaded Afghanistan, conflating the Afghan Taliban with the primarily Arab internationalist al-Qaeda. The Taliban were driven from Afghanistan by December 2001,

---

[32] A combined total of roughly 50,000 (15,000 dead and 35,000 wounded). Not included in the total are approximately 2 million Afghans dead, mostly civilian.

with most of the survivors initially fleeing to largely Pashtun areas of Pakistan. Since then, U.S. and other foreign military forces have maintained a presence in Afghanistan to suppress the Taliban and al-Qaeda and assure the survival of a "sort of democratic" Kabul-based government. As of 2019, this effort does not seem to be prospering with a resurgence of Taliban, al-Qaeda, and the creation of an even more violently extreme organization called Islamic State-Khorasan Province (IS-KP).

The point of reviewing the previous roughly 300 years of history associated with the area we call Afghanistan today is to show that any assumption that this geographically isolated, backwater area is of little importance is a gross mistake. Afghanistan and its inhabitants should be ignored at one's peril, as they have shown a propensity to reach beyond their borders—however that can be achieved—to bring death, destruction, and vast global restructurings.

Opium as a Transformative Agent

One of the major reasons for the recent prolonged resistance of Afghan insurgent groups and supporting foreign Islamic fighters and a major cause of the failure of the Kabul-based government is the rapid growth of opium planting, harvesting, and trafficking. Opium has been grown in Afghanistan for centuries, but it was a localized product, with most commercially marketed opium originating in India or elsewhere. During the Soviet occupation, Afghanistan state control diminished and insurgents began growing opium to finance insurgent acquisition of weapons and support—combined, these two consequences of occupation inspired a significant uptick in opium growth. Moreover, during civil war, with the prominence of local warlords and few tangible resources to barter with, opium growth skyrocketed. By 2000, despite an advertised Taliban antiopium campaign, opium trafficking out of Afghanistan went global.

Today, opium farming has taken root in Afghanistan as the primary cash crop, and trafficking with its concurrent corruption and erosion of effective governance is an existential threat to the current Afghan government and possibly its tenuous status as a state. Moreover, these problems exacerbate threats to the religious and moral integrity of the Taliban. If research coming out of organizations such as the United Nations is correct, as of 2019, approximately 80 percent of all opium grown globally is sourced from Afghanistan, from which almost 90 percent of heroin production is drawn from. To provide greater context, 40 percent of opium worldwide comes from Helmand Province alone.[33] The result is millions of opium addicts in Afghanistan, Pakistan, China, Iran, Russia, and beyond. These hard facts are driving Russia and Iran to negotiate with the Taliban, who do not tolerate opium addicts within their ranks and have shown a marked ability to control the flow of opium. These actions simultaneously withdraw legitimacy from the Kabul-based Afghan government and provide the Taliban with political legitimacy. With a politically and militarily stronger Taliban, the United States decided to raise U.S. force levels in Afghanistan from 8,500 to possibly 14,000 or more.[34]

Religious versus Ethnic Narrative

Within the context discussed to this point, it only gets more complicated, because if the question is asked (and it is), What is the strategic culture of Afghanistan today?—this author would have to respond by asking: Which one? While the historical review, combined with the ethnicity puzzle has been depict-

---

[33] See *Afghanistan Opium Survey, 2016: Cultivation and Production* (Vienna: UN Office on Drugs and Crime, Islamic Republic of Afghanistan, Ministry of Counter Narcotics, 2016). An astounding 37 percent of global opium comes from Sangin District in Helmand Province.

[34] See David Nakamura and Abby Phillip, "Trump Announces New Strategy for Afghanistan that Calls for a Troop Increase," *Washington Post*, 21 August 2017.

ed by this chapter, one needs to add to this brew another key variable—religion. The primary religion of Afghanistan is Islam, with approximately 85 percent of the population being Sunni Muslim. The Shia minority is almost completely Hazara (see map 1), with a tiny slice of Pashtuns located in eastern Afghanistan (a handful of Turi tribesmen mostly in extreme eastern Paktia and Khost provinces). In addition, there are approximately 200,000 Nuristanis in Nuristan Province, approximately 10,000 Zoroastrians (followers of a pre-Islamic religion) in far western Afghanistan, and minute pockets of Hindus (about 1,000) and an unknown number of Baloch Zikri Muslims (a.k.a. Mahdavia).[35] It is therefore clear that, while Afghanistan has a main religion, most Afghans practice Islam in different ways and there are further conflicts with those who are considered outside of the mainstream religion.

The Pashtuns of Afghanistan (and Pakistan) follow an unwritten moral and ethical code that provides extensive rules and guidance for their behavior(s) and lifestyle(s). It has existed since at least the 1st millennium BCE.[36] This system of law and governance emphasizes the personal responsibility of Pashtuns to continually explore its essence and meaning. It is interpreted as the way of the Pashtun. It is practiced widely among rural Pashtuns, which are the majority, and less so among those in urban areas. It has also been adopted among some non-Pashtuns, generally those who live among or near Pashtuns. As it has been present for so long, it has and does pose a direct challenge to Islam, which is a complete religious ideology on

---

[35] Mainly of Dardic descent, they follow a variety of localized Indo-Iranian polytheistic practices and have been the subject of numerous Sunni jihads for the last 250 years or so. The author conducted several negotiations with the Nuristanis and learned of the Sunni Pashtun jihadi practices in person.

[36] For more, see Samir Nath, *Dictionary of Vedanta* (New Delhi: Sarup & Sons, 2002); and Marlijn T. Houtsma et al., eds., *E. J. Brill's First Encyclopaedia of Islam, 1913–1936*, vol. IV (Leiden, Netherlands: E. J. Brill, 1993).

how to live one's life. When Islam was introduced by way of war (jihad) in the late 600s, it was resisted fiercely by Pashtuns, who rallied around the Pashtunwali (unwritten ethical code). It was not until the 1100s that Islam became the major faith of many Pashtuns, and Islam was the single major remaining religion in Afghanistan only once the Mongols in the 1220s and then the armies of Tamerlane in the 1380s managed to exterminate Zoroastrianism, Buddhism, Christianity, and Hinduism. Still, the struggle to convert continues in northeastern Afghanistan even today, aimed at the non-Pashtun Nuristani peoples who live adjacent to the Pashtuns.

Today, Islam is the overwhelming religious faith of most Afghans, yet it conflicts in many ways with the Pashtunwali. Other ethnic groups have similar or related "codes" such as the Balochmayar and the Turkmenchiliki, yet almost all Afghans, even those not Pashtun, are familiar with much of the Pashtunwali. The treatment of Afghans versus the treatment of Muslims in the case of killing is one conflict (revenge versus no harm to fellow Muslims), as is the treatment and status of women (with Islam being the much more tolerant "system"). There are enough significant differences between the Pashtunwali and the religion of Islam to create cultural confusion, which can be exploited and calls into question which strategic culture (or narrative) one should consider when operating in Afghanistan.

These religious differences have noticeable impact, depending on what the individual Afghan chooses to identify with. If an Afghan wants to identify with a specific ethnicity, that would presuppose an increasing awareness of the Pashtun plurality working hard for "Pashtunization" of all Afghans, something underway since Emir Abdur Rahman Khan's rule in 1880–1901, which saw the slaughter of more than 50 percent of the Hazara population then. Despite an acceptance by all ethnic groups within Afghanistan, the Pashtunization effort has not been notably successful when separate from genocidal methods of rule (something the Taliban would like to bring back) as the language of governance is still Dari (a close variant of Farsi spoken mainly by Tajiks).

If an Afghan chooses an identity based on religion, that presents several options as most Afghans are illiterate and depend on illiterate or semiliterate mullahs (religious leaders) for their guidance. There are essentially two options for a religious Sunni Afghan: one is Salafism, which can lead to the preoccupation with preventing taghut so as not to upset religious leaders or rulers, dissatisfaction with the government, and a trend toward the Taliban (or more recently toward IS-KP). Alternatively, Sunni Afghans can also pursue the influence and moderation that is espoused by Sufism and its practices. All of this is a gross simplification, but it needs to be noted.[37]

Informal Security-based Institutions

Considering several factors to this point—Afghanistan's long history, the role of opium, and religious and ethnic differences —it is clear that Afghanistan might be a state but not a unified state. Therefore, an Afghan as an individual is a composite of several identities based on ethnicity, tribal affiliation, religion or sect membership, and region. Afghanistan, or the region we recognize as Afghanistan today, has traditionally not been under centralized control but under extremely devolved, or decentralized, rule.

---

[37] *Taghut* is an Arabic term for the following: the three-letter Arabic verbal root of ط-غ-ت T-G-T, which means to "cross the limits, overstep boundaries" or "to rebel." From this, taghut denotes one who exceeds their limits. This notion is associated with the three stages of disbelief in the Islamic context. The first stage of error is *fisq* (i.e., disobeying God without denying that one should obey), the second is *kufr* (i.e., rejection of the very idea that one should obey God). The last stage would be not only to rebel against God but also impose their rebellion against the will of God upon others. Those who reach this stage are considered as taghut. Taghut can be associated with Salafism, which is all about preventing taghut.

When looking for a strategic culture in Afghanistan, it is fairly accurate to say that any definition would have to take into account security institutions (tribal, dynastic, invading) that typify a significant emphasis on militarized culture at the lowest levels and intimate knowledge with the utility (both positively and negatively) of force. The two major competing ideologies—Islam and the Pashtunwali—are constantly competing with how to resolve disputes at all levels, peacefully or not, which creates confusion in identifying such a strategic culture. Regional order has always been important to those who reside within Afghanistan, with an apparent preference of organized forces to enforce peace. Additionally, that same preference for security through the use of force is influenced by the massive instabilities created by Persian, British, and Russian imperial intervention, Soviet invasion, U.S./Coalition intervention, and the pervasively corrupting glut of opium.

Kin Networks

Still, Afghans have developed an institutional device that might be at least the outline for a strategic culture, or perhaps something less than strategic culture—a strategic narrative. As amply depicted above, Afghans self-divide and do so even more granularly than discussed to this point. At the foundation of this division is not the tribe or ethnicity but the family, all of whom live in extended kinship networks. Expansion and growth of such networks leads to the development of clans and ultimately tribes (or for Tajiks, regionally based identities, such as Panjshiris, Badakhshi, or Andarabi).[38] Afghans can and often do unite, however. Despite ethnic, tribal, or religious differences, Afghans will, when a threat arises that threatens all, come together employing a social-cultural device called the "manteqa."

---

[38] Pierre Centlivres and Micheline Centlivres-Demont, "The Invention of the Afghan Nationalities, 1980–2004," Middle East Institute, 18 April 2012.

The Manteqa

In addition to tribe or place or region where a person comes from or lives, the manteqa is another element shaping identity in Afghanistan. While other factors seem to divide Afghans, the manteqa builds solidarity into society and provides a foundation for considering how Afghanistan, as a nation-state, pursues its strategic culture. The manteqa is possibly the actual social and territorial unit of rural Afghanistan, but it is not reflected in formal governance structures such as districts or provinces. Commonly, a manteqa is composed of several villages or a cluster of villages where solidarity is shaped among the local population; higher- and national-level identities are only used in the advent of real or potential overwhelming threat. These manteqa do not have any administrative recognition, although traditional structures and committees exist at the manteqa level (i.e., *shura-e manteqa*, *rish safedan-e manteqa*, *nomayendagan-e manteqa*, or *shura-e mahali*).[39] The manteqa and their committees are the missing interactive links between the federal, provincial, or district administration and the kin-

---

[39] The definition of community is complicated in an Afghan context. There are various terms in regards to the loci of rural community life, in addition to the term *manteqa*, which approximately means "area." These other terms can be used or included under manteqa, those being *qarya* (usually translated as village) and *qishlaq* (settlement). None of these concepts have a standard administrative definition within the current local unit of government in Afghanistan, the district (woluswali). A district contains many qarya, qishlaq, and manteqa, yet none are formally associated with the district council or municipal administrative center. However, despite not having any formal administrative designation, the traditional institutional structures of manteqa, qishlaq, and qarya, normally called shuras (e.g., shura-e manteqa, shura-e qishlaq, or shura-e qarya, all of which are informal governing structures versus having any religious connotation), typically resolve conflicts over rangeland and agricultural land rights (village chakbashi, mirab, and zamindar can play key roles here, often with a respected mullah or sufi pir playing the mediator) within a given manteqa. For more on this, see Raphy Favre, *Interface between State and Society in Afghanistan: Discussion on Key Social Features Affecting Governance, Reconciliation and Reconstruction* (Addis Ababa, Ethiopia: AIZON, 2005).

based village. The manteqa committees, part of an informal governance system and based on the Pashtunwali, are called jirgas. *Jirgas*, literally meaning circle to emphasize the complete equality of all Pashtun men, are normally used for resolving major tribal or interclan issues, such as conflict, land disputes, or serious crimes. As such, it is secular in nature and not based on religion, making it ideal for the manteqa.

Examples of how manteqa are used are numerous and encompass a wide range of threats from environmental to geopolitical. Security-wise, if Afghanistan is invaded by powerful outsiders (say, the Soviet Union) and most or all Afghans recognize that threat, divisive routines are dispensed with and most unite to fight the invader. If there is a natural disaster, such as a massive flood on the Helmand-Arghandab river system, everybody unites or they die. It is also used in peacetime, primarily to address water resource issues, which are an ongoing general threat to health and survival. For example, almost all water issues in Afghanistan are handled via this device and not by the government, aside from a few major projects. Coincidentally, when Afghanistan has attempted major projects through the government instead of the manteqa, such as the Helmand and Arghandab Valley Authority, they have been well-meaning and ambitious but not done well. Here are several examples of successfully using manteqa for water management at various levels:

Wakil *and* mirab-bashi *(interprovincial manteqa)— for overall management, conflict resolution, scheduling annual maintenance, coordinating* hashar *(communal unpaid labor), collection of annual contributions, coordinating emergency response, and external coordination*

Mirab *and* chakbashi *(drainage basin manteqa)— management of branch water allocation and rotation, coordinating annual maintenance, and conflict resolution*

Mirab *and* chakbashi *(inter- and intradistrict man-*

teqa)—managing system operation, supervising annual maintenance, supervising construction works, and collection of annual contributions

Zamindar/Mirab *Canal Committee (village-level manteqa)—management of water allocation and provision of* hashar *labor for maintenance*

It should be noted that, within all the above examples of water management using the manteqa device, security concerns (e.g., conflict resolution, communal labor, and collecting contributions) dominate. These instruments and resulting institutions are the foundation of the strategic culture of Afghanistan but exist outside of established governance structures. Any entity, however, that desires to exert political control and security over the area of Afghanistan depends upon this nongovernmental structure, often unwittingly.

As a side note, there has been an extensive amount of publishing done on Afghanistan, writings that refer to the region as an "ungoverned space," either in part or in whole. The above outline should put that tendentious view to rest. In some ways, it could be said that Afghanistan has an overabundance of governance at the village level.[40]

Conclusion

Depending on who is asking and who is answering, describing what the current strategic culture of Afghanistan is can bring various and often conflicting responses. Clearly, there is an emphasis on security, be it the Kabul government, Taliban, IS-KP, or outsiders such as Russia, Iran, Pakistan, or the United States, who also want security and control to prevent crossborder drug flow, insurgency actions, refugee migration, instability, etc. While Afghanistan could be a near-failed state, the historical

---

[40] Keister, "The Illusion of Chaos."

record suggests that it directly influences not only surrounding countries but also many countries across the globe. Afghanistan is important, given its location and terrain, even though perhaps it should not be. Maybe it is—as Milton Bearden called it in 2001—a "graveyard of empires." Or one might even argue that Afghanistan can be called the "destroyer of empires."[41]

In fact, an argument can be made that Afghanistan should not even be a state, because it was not much more than a buffer space between established states maintained to keep empires from clashing during the era of the Great Game. Yet, Afghanistan has been and remains a state with a national identity, even though it can be depicted, with apologies to Samuel P. Huntington, as a clash of minicivilizations.[42] While Afghanistan might not fit into the traditional categories that Western thinkers use, and on which foreign policy analysts rely, viewing the nation through the lens of strategic culture has value. Asking questions about Afghanistan's strategic culture answers some questions and raises others but, in the end, the questions themselves demonstrate how differently Americans think about problems of security and responses to them as compared to Afghans. Moreover, Americans need to be aware, when trying to find commonalities among Afghans, how diverse Afghans are themselves. Considering the endurance of Afghanistan despite invasion, intervention, occupation, and even genocide, it has continued to defy Western solutions to security. It seems clear that asking more questions about Afghanistan, as we have done here, may be more important than what the current answers are.

---

[41] For more, see Milton Bearden, "Afghanistan, Graveyard of Empires," *Foreign Affairs*, November/December 2001.

[42] In reference to Samuel P. Huntington, "The Clash of Civilizations?," *Foreign Affairs*, Summer 1993. The term has also been used by Bernard Lewis, "The Roots of Muslim Rage," *Atlantic Monthly*, September 1990; and Basil Mathews, *Young Islam on Trek: A Study in the Clash of Civilizations* (Whitefish, MT: Kessinger Publishing, 2007), 196.

CHAPTER
4

BRAZILIAN STRATEGIC CULTURE AND THE AMAZON

by Denise Slater

Brazil maintains a long history of partnership with the United States that started in 1826 and became more significant after World War II.[1] This chapter will explore some aspects of Brazilian strategic culture that are relevant to understanding how Brazil perceives threats and their major security concerns, especially in relation to the Amazon region. This understanding is particularly important for U.S. policy makers, government officials, and military personnel who regularly engage in diplomatic or security cooperation activities with Brazilians.

After a brief discussion of Brazilian strategic culture themes, this chapter will outline the two main institutional players in Brazil that have historically helped create, shape, and maintain strategic culture: the diplomatic corps and the military. The analysis will focus on the case study of the Amazon region that is center stage in Brazilian strategic culture. It will also present the processes by which these key players, and in particular the armed forces, have interwoven their long-lasting security

---

[1] William R. Manning, "An Early Diplomatic Controversy between the United States and Brazil," *American Journal of International Law* 12, no. 2 (April 1918): 291–311, http://doi.org/10.2307/2188145.

132

sensitivities—or strategic culture elements—into the national defense strategy. Once incorporated into the national defense strategy, these strategic culture elements trickled down to military doctrine and into military organizational culture. This process allowed for the strengthening of these themes promoted by the military, as these achieved a permanent status into a defense strategy that was broadly vetted by civil society. This magnified their reach and their scope, but it also consolidated their permanence into Brazil's policy making and institutions.

When writing about nations that may present a clear threat or danger to the United States, authors frequently focus on strategic culture themes that will give a broader understanding of a nation's motivations for action, its cultural peculiarities on security, or may even attempt to predict that country's future behavior in certain situations. Therefore, the strategic culture definitions used for these studies are often broad, thorough, and as all-encompassing as possible. Other authors have included an additional layer, expanding the study's scope from international relations into other social sciences, such as psychology and anthropology. Colin S. Gray endorsed Jack L. Snyder's 1977 definition of strategic culture, which illustrates this conceptual broadening:

> the sum total of ideas, conditioned emotional responses, and patterns of habitual behavior that members of a national strategic community have acquired through instruction or imitation and share with each other with regard to [nuclear] strategy.[2]

This definition is central to this study, as well as Nayef al-Rodhan's, who contributes to an expanded view of strategic culture, one that encompasses "the emotionality of states (national pride and prestige) and the egoism of states (the pursuit

---

[2] Gray, *Out of the Wilderness*, 9.

of national interests)."[3] Both definitions highlight the relevance of emotionality as a key element of strategic culture and both provide insights for understanding Brazilian strategic culture, particularly regarding the Amazon region.[4]

The *emotionality of states* approach, seemingly irrational to an outside observer, may illuminate the internal thinking of key governmental institutions and agencies, which are reflected in their organizational culture. Organizational culture is a topic that has been studied by various disciplines and through many approaches, and therefore it has no single widely accepted definition. For this study, *organizational culture* will be understood as "the taken-for-granted values, underlying assumptions, expectations, collective memories, and definitions present in an organization."[5] Organizational culture, in this context, will be used to shed light on the behavior of key institutional players—in this case, the Brazilian military. The analysis will include the processes that have resulted in the implementation of emotional elements of strategic culture into the organizational culture of the armed forces. Once consolidated in the national strategy, these elements upgraded doctrine and were thus incorporated into the military's organizational culture. As the military continued to execute guidelines set forth by the new doctrine, these new patterns of behaviors were consolidated and strengthened in "conditioned emotional responses," as described by Gray.[6]

Therefore, observing these processes can ultimately help

---

[3] Nayef al-Rodhan, "Strategic Culture and Pragmatic National Interest," *Global Policy*, 22 July 2015.

[4] Russell D. Howard, *Strategic Culture*, JSOU Report 13-8 (MacDill Air Force Base, FL: Joint Special Operations University, 2013), 2; Gray, *Out of the Wilderness*, 14; and al-Rodhan, "Strategic Culture and Pragmatic National Interest."

[5] Kim S. Cameron and Robert E. Quinn, *Diagnosing and Changing Organizational Culture: Based on the Competing Values Framework* (Reading, MA: Addison-Wesley, 1999), 14. See also Stephen J. Gerras et al., *Organizational Culture: Applying a Hybrid Model to the U.S. Army* (Carlisle, PA: U.S. Army War College, 2008), 2.

[6] Gray, *Out of the Wilderness*, 9.

U.S. government institutions and agencies that regularly engage with Brazilian military and civilian institutions to better understand the Brazilian armed forces' organizational culture. In short, this case study will provide an additional layer for the understanding of certain emotional, unexpected, or seemingly irrational responses on the part of key decision-making Brazilian institutions that influence strategy, especially concerning the Amazon region. Specifically, this case study will shed light on two main issues. The first issue will address how the Brazilian military, and to a lesser extent the diplomatic corps, inserted certain themes and elements of strategic culture that shaped Brazilian national defense policies. These elements of strategic culture promoted by the military refer primarily to the strategic relevance of the Amazon. These views reflect a strong nationalism in relation to the Amazon as well as the consolidation of geopolitical views that combine *nationalism, modernization*, and *development* of the Amazon. These themes and others will be detailed in the sections below. The second issue addressed is how these ideas have guided military doctrine and influenced the organizational culture of the armed forces once they were incorporated into policy.

Why would this be relevant to U.S. policy makers or to government officials and military personnel engaged with their Brazilian counterparts? Many of the political, religious, and cultural differences between the United States and Iran, or the United States and North Korea, are evident due to polarized and antagonistic worldviews. The differences are so marked that it is expected that cultural sensitivities could trigger emotional responses from these states. These cultural sensitivities could also be triggered by certain topics or elements of strategic culture. However, when dealing with friendly, partner nations such as Brazil, which is a democratic nation that shares many similar cultural values, these cultural sensitivities that could trigger the emotionality of the state are not as easily understood and may be more subtle. Nevertheless, there are topics or elements of strategic culture that could trigger the emotionality of these states as well. These potentially hot-button issues are embedded as an intrinsic part of the elements of strategic culture of all states. This case study shows how these elements of strategic culture make their way into the organizational cultures of the primary shapers of strategic culture in Brazil. Strategic culture may provide American policy makers or military personnel additional insights into how a partner nation might react when dealing with sensitive topics related to strategic culture or to its elements. This kind of insight could help them avoid unnecessary strains in relations resulting from miscommunication or misunderstanding.

The Primary Shapers of Brazilian Strategic Culture

Historically, the armed forces and the Brazilian Ministry of Foreign Affairs (Ministério das Relações Exteriores)—also known as *Itamaraty*—have been the most influential and stable institutions in Brazil, and because of this they have the most influence on strategic culture.[7] The Brazilian military is one of the few governmental organizations in Brazil that is highly trusted by the public; according to one study, the military have a 68.1 percent approval rating, with similar or higher averages by other polls.[8] Consequently, their actions and perceptions with regard to strategic culture reverberates throughout Brazilian society. A high rate of approval by civil society contrasts sharply with low trust in political institutions, a trend that continues to

---

[7] Luis Bitencourt and Alcides Costa Vaz, *Brazilian Strategic Culture* (Miami: Florida International University Applied Research Center, 2009), 5.

[8] Daniel Montalvo, "Do You Trust Your Armed Forces?," *AmericasBarometer Insights*, no. 27 (2009); and Guilherme Russo, "Amid Brazil's Crises: Low and Declining Respect for Political Institutions," *Americas Barometer Topical Brief*, 1 April 2016, 4.

spiral down as multiple corruption scandals undermine public trust in politicians and state institutions.[9]

The Brazilian diplomatic corps, along with the military, also enjoy a high rate of public approval. Since the late nineteenth century, when the Brazilian borders were consolidated through peaceful negotiations, Itamaraty enjoyed the reputation of a world-class diplomatic corps and is a respected institution among Brazilians. Therefore, while in other countries, where leaders of religious groups, political parties, castes, ethnicities, or social classes are key to creating the strategic culture of their nations, the military and diplomatic leadership are central to the formation of Brazilian strategic culture. As in most nations, neither the culture nor the creators of it exist in a vacuum, and Brazilian history explains how these two groups became the primary influencers of Brazilian strategic culture.[10]

The Origins of Diplomatic Identity

José Maria da Silva Paranhos, known as the Baron of Rio Branco (1845–1912), was the most renowned diplomat in Brazilian history and the patron of Brazilian diplomatic corps.[11] As a diplomat and a historian, the baron masterfully settled Brazilian border disputes—many times resorting to international arbitration—but without the need to engage in military confrontation or all-out war. However, the baron still supported the existence of a strong deterrence, as he once proclaimed: "No State can be peaceful without being strong. It is very good

---

[9] Russo, "Amid Brazil's Crises," 4.

[10] Luigi R. Einaudi, "Brazil and the United States: The Need for Strategic Engagement," *Strategic Forum—National Defense University*, SF No. 266 (March 2011): 5.

[11] "Biografia: Barao do Rio Branco (Jose Maria da Silva Paranhos)," Academia Brasileira de Letras, accessed 6 July 2017.

to discuss treaties while having behind you a credible fleet."[12]

The baron's successful negotiation skills benefited Brazil on numerous occasions and earned him the accolade of "father" of Itamaraty. His successful negotiations solidified the reputation of Itamaraty, both nationally and internationally. Therefore, Brazilian foreign policy has historically promoted Brazil's identity as a peaceful nation. This identity has manifested itself throughout Brazilian diplomatic and military culture. For example, there is a strong belief that peace should always be pursued first, prizing negotiation and accommodation to avoid conflict. Over time, this cultural trait consolidated into an identifiable trait in Brazilian diplomacy, as Brazil always supports international multilateralism, favoring pacifist dispute resolutions, respect for principles of sovereign equality, non-interventionism, international legal frameworks, and human rights. These themes have evolved and became a part of the zeitgeist of national culture. In his inaugural class to students at the Brazilian diplomatic academy, the former defense minister, Raul Jungmann (2016–18), said that Brazil lives by the "mantra of soft power" and that "the nation represents a powerhouse of peace." Additionally, he claimed that Brazil suffers "no threats" and presently has "no enemies."[13] From the baron to Jungmann, Brazilian diplomats have pursued a century of peace that suits the nation's cultural and social values.[14]

Other elements of this peaceful identity can be traced back to colonial times (1500–1822). Brazilian colonial history contrasts with the history of colonial Spanish America in four crucial ways. First, unlike the Spanish conquistadors, the Por-

---

[12] Raul Jungmann, "Aula Inaugural proferida pelo Ministro de Estado da Defesa" [Inaugural lecture given by the Minister of Defense] (lecture, Instituto Rio Branco, Brasilia, DF, 25 January 2017), slide 7.

[13] Jungmann, "Aula Inaugural proferida pelo Ministro de Estado da Defesa," slide 10.

[14] Jungmann, "Aula Inaugural proferida pelo Ministro de Estado da Defesa," slide 10.

tuguese colonizers were neither warriors nor Christian noblemen. Moreover, the Portuguese colonizers, as opposed to their Spanish counterparts, did not have to fight advanced civilizations, such as the Incas and Aztecs. Second, at the time of the Portuguese exploration of South America in 1500, there was no organized widespread indigenous society in the land that became Brazil; there were only scattered tribes of hunters and gatherers, such as the Tupí Guarani and Tapuias, living on a foraging existence. In sharp contrast with the experience of the Spanish in the Americas, there was no gold or silver found in Brazil for the first hundred years, making Brazil less profitable than the Spanish American colonies.[15] Third, Portugal did not possess the same financial and military power as the Spanish, which made it more difficult to keep a tight grip on its American colony as had the Spanish. Fourth, the Brazilian independence from Portugal was relatively bloodless and nonviolent. This historical narrative of peaceful nation building formed a key feature of Brazil's enduring strategic culture.

The Brazilian path to independence contrasts sharply from Spanish America's violent wars of independence from Spain. When the Portuguese court fled from Napoleon's forces that invaded Iberia in 1807, the British Royal Navy escorted the Portuguese court to Rio de Janeiro. The court settled in Rio de Janeiro from 1808 to 1821, and its presence brought unprecedented progress to the colony. Portuguese Prince Regent João VI (1769–1826) and more than 10,000 officials moved to Rio de Janeiro, which became the capital of the Portuguese empire for the next 13 years. The son of the king of Portugal, Dom Pedro I, declared Brazilian independence from Portugal in 1822, which was achieved in a relatively simple and easy manner. Moreover, it did not encounter

---

[15] Rex A. Hudson, ed., "The Indigenous Population," in *Brazil: A Country Study* (Washington, DC: Federal Research Division, Library of Congress, 1997); and Thomas E. Skidmore et al., *Modern Latin America*, 3d ed. (Oxford, UK: Oxford University Press, 1992), 24.

much significant opposition from the Portuguese crown or from the Portuguese merchants who benefited economically from the status quo. While the opposing sides engaged in some scattered guerrilla confrontations, occasional demonstrations occurred, and plenty of political maneuvering took place, both sides avoided outright conflict.[16]

The Brazilian Military

Brazil's history also explains why its military plays a key role in shaping strategic culture. After independence, Brazil spent the next 67 years as a peaceful empire. The first emperor, Dom Pedro I, was forced to leave for Portugal, for dynastic reasons. His son, Pedro II, enjoyed a long reign, which was only interrupted by the Paraguayan War (1864–70), until being deposed in 1889, which to this day was Brazil's largest war. The Paraguayan War, also known as the War of the Triple Alliance, gave the Brazilian Army its main battle experience, and its only war in the nineteenth century.[17] While some countries deemphasize the military after war, in the case of Brazil, the war helped bring the military into important political and cultural roles.

The war provided the Brazilian Army with iconic military heroes, allowed for the rapid expansion from 17,000 personnel to 100,000, cemented close relations with Argentina, and fixed the main operations on the southern borders for decades to come. The war also had a deep and lasting effect on politics within Brazil, with officers becoming important actors in Brazilian politics, which led to the creation of the Republican movement in Brazil in the 1870s. The Republicans were abolitionists and were behind the political effort that culminated

---

[16] Hudson, "The Kingdom of Portugal and Brazil, 1815–21," in *Brazil*; and Hudson, "The Second Empire, 1840–89," in *Brazil*.

[17] Dannin M. Hanratty and Sandra W. Meditz, eds., "The War of the Triple Alliance," in *Paraguay: A Country Study* (Washington, DC: Federal Research Division, Library of Congress, 1988).

with eliminating slavery in Brazil. On 13 May 1888, Princess Isabel Cristina de Bragança e Bourbon d'Orléans (daughter of Dom Pedro II) signed the Golden Law, which by a strike of her plume literally abolished slavery in Brazil. With the military's support, the Republican party led a political movement that also put an end to the monarchy in 1889.[18] Amid a political crisis, Field Marshal Manuel Deodoro da Fonseca proclaimed the republic. Since then, the Brazilian military has been part of the country's ruling elite and is deeply involved in the shaping of Brazilian strategic culture.

Another important event that shaped Brazil's military strategic culture occurred during the interwar and World War II era. Brazil faced a series of political crises in the 1930s and 1940s that included Communist insurgency, revolutionary uprisings, and military interventions. The period was particularly marked by the presidency and the dictatorship of Getulio Vargas (1930–45 and 1951–54), a period known as *Estado Novo* ("The New State"). Vargas led Brazil during the polarization between Communism and fascism, a historical period that closely resembled fascism in Brazil.[19] But it was a representative of the diplomatic corps—Brazil's former foreign minister and former ambassador to the United States and a close friend to Vargas, Oswaldo Aranha (1894–1960)—who convinced Vargas to join the Allies in the war. Even though Vargas eventually followed Oswaldo Aranha's advice, Brazil was late but joined the Allies in the fight against Germany and Italy in 1944.[20]

Even though Brazil joined the Allied forces late in the war,

---

[18] Hudson, "The Second Empire," *Brazil*; and Skidmore et al., *Modern Latin America*, 149–50.

[19] "Diretrizes do Estado Novo (1937–1945); Estado Novo e Fascismo," Centro de Pesquisa e Documentação de História Contemporânea do Brasil (CPDOC)—Escola de Ciências Sociais da Fundação Getulio Vargas, accessed 15 August 2017.

[20] Rollie E. Poppino, "Getulio Vargas," Encyclopædia Britannica, 15 April 2019; and "Biografias: Oswaldo Aranha" [Biographies: Oswaldo Aranha], UOL, accessed 6 July 2017.

the country did provide essential raw materials to Allied air and naval bases. In 1944, Brazil sent a combat division of 25,000 troops to Italy that fought alongside the U.S. Fifth Army during the Allied invasion. Vargas negotiated for some benefits with the United States in exchange for providing raw materials and bases. He also raised the Amazon's strategic wartime importance, which resulted in successful exchange of economic and technical assistance from the U.S. government to advance long-term development goals in the Amazon region. Vargas's regime laid the groundwork for the government's public policies in the Amazon for decades to come, especially during the military rule, from 1964 to 1985.[21]

During the Cold War, an era when the world was characterized by two antagonistic regimes, the Brazilian military sided ideologically with the United States. However, in 1964, Brazilian democracy began to disintegrate. The country was engulfed in the political chaos posed by the threat of a Cuban Revolution–inspired Communist insurrection. As historian Thomas Skidmore described,

> *The populist policies of Getulio Vargas constructed a hierarchical order through which the state created and controlled institutions for organizing urban workers. This posed a significant, but ultimately unacceptable challenge to the upper and middle classes, the latter largely represented by the military.*[22]

The urban guerrillas' goal was to install a Communist state in Brazil, a proposal that clashed with the military. The military seized power and controlled the country for 21 years, leading

---

[21] Skidmore and Smith, *Modern Latin America*, 168; and Seth Garfield, *In Search of the Amazon: Brazil, the United States, and the Nature of a Region* (Durham, NC: Duke University Press, 2013), 205, 201.

[22] Skidmore and Smith, *Modern Latin America*, 178.

the country through a progressive, bureaucratic-authoritarian regime.[23]

The Concept of Grandeza

During the 1970s and 1980s, the military forged an ideology that combined nationalism, modernization, and development that has continued to influence civilians and politicians alike. The centerpiece of their ideology was based on the concept of *grandeza* (greatness), which is the enduring belief that Brazil is destined to be great and that it has everything it needs to become a great power. This geopolitical deterministic belief was well developed by General Golbery do Couto e Silva (1911–87) in his 1967 book titled *Geopolítica do Brasil* (Brazil's Geopolitics). His ideas as expressed in the book heavily influenced the army during the military regime.[24] The Amazon's strategic relevance was central to his geopolitical thinking. As previously mentioned, the Amazon's importance was boosted by the Vargas regime during WWII, which resulted in economic and technical assistance from the U.S. government to advance long-term development goals in the Amazon region.

General Carlos de Meira Mattos was another author who also influenced military thinking in that time, especially regarding the Amazon. Like General Golbery, General Mattos also highlighted the importance of integrating the vast Amazon rainforest and basin with the rest of the country. Together, they made an imprint regarding the geopolitical component of grandeza, focusing on the certainty that Brazil was destined to be a superpower because of its immense and largely untapped natural resources.

In 1979, the military regime responded to political pressures for democratization by allowing for the creation of multiple

---

[23] Skidmore and Smith, *Modern Latin America*, 178.
[24] Golbery do Couto e Silva, *Geopolítica do Brasil* (Brazil: José Olympio, 1967).

opposition parties.[25] These opposition parties gained momentum in the late 1980s, coinciding with the broader, worldwide movements for the end of Cold War, which prepared the way for the military to allow for the return of democracy to Brazil in 1985. In the early 1990s, after democracy was reinstated, the military's direct political influence diminished, and though they were castigated by sharp budget cuts, their capacity to shape strategic culture did not subside. Nevertheless, after a 21-year military rule, the role of the armed forces dramatically changed in Brazil. After the redemocratization process began, the armed forces peacefully handed power back to civilians. Since then, the Brazilian military has been under the authority of an antimilitary, populist, socialist-oriented executive branch, a period that ended in 2018 with the election of Jair Messias Bolsonaro, a conservative former army captain who is highly supportive of the military. Notwithstanding, the prior two decades also coincided with one of the most severe economic crises that engulfed Latin America.

The crisis affected many countries in the region, especially Brazil, and included hyperinflation, the erosion of income, the decline of the middle class, and a sharp reduction in savings for all citizens. During the same period, the new congress deeply cut military expenditures and military pay. The military withdrawal from power coincided with an economic downturn, resulting in deeper budget cuts for the military. Because Brazil was already among the countries with the lowest levels of military expenditures, those cuts sharply affected military readiness and morale.[26] Nevertheless, despite the military's declining political influence and drastic cuts to its budget, it retained many prerogatives and remained a major actor on many issues,

---

[25] "Governos Militares no Brasil (continuação)," Sohistoria, accessed 5 September 2017.
[26] "Brazil: Defense Spending," GlobalSecurity, accessed 6 July 2017.

including being one of the major strategic culture players in the nation.[27]

The Search for a New Role and Mission for the Armed Forces

In 1999, the new civilian administration created the Ministry of Defense (MOD), combining the army, the air force, and the navy under civilian command. As the administration and the Brazilian armed forces searched for new missions and a redefined role in society, it became clear that Brazil needed a new national defense strategy. During the reshaping of national defense priorities, resuming deployment of Brazilian troops to United Nations (UN) peacekeeping missions was something that the Brazilian armed forces welcomed wholeheartedly. The 2005 UN peacekeeping mission in Haiti, called the United Nations Stabilization Mission in Haiti (Mission des Nations Unies pour la Stabilisation en Haïti [MINUSTAH]), offered the Brazilian military the perfect opportunity to modernize its outdated equipment, boost salaries, acquire training, and align the military with the civilian government's strategy.[28]

This new direction, in the form of a UN peacekeeping mission strategy, improved the country's international standing and paid off in multiple areas. MINUSTAH provided the Brazilian military with much-needed training for their troops. Brazilian battalions conducted regular patrols and raids to pacify the most violent neighborhoods in Haiti, such as Cité Soleil. Upon their return to Brazil, the military used this training to launch similar cleanup operations in the crime-ridden

---

[27] Scott D. Tollefson, "Civil-Military Relations in Brazil: The Myth of Tutelary Democracy" (paper presented at the 1995 meeting of the Latin American Studies Association, Sheraton, Washington, DC, 28–30 September 1995).

[28] "Estrategia Nacional de Defesa" [National defense strategy], Ministerio da Defesa [Ministry of Defense], accessed 6 July 2017; and "United Nations Peacekeeping," United Nations, 21 November 2016, accessed 6 July 2017.

slums of Rio de Janeiro. The Brazilian government purchased new equipment from the Brazilian defense sector to support the army's participation in MINUSTAH, providing a considerable boost to the defense industry.[29]

Diplomatic and Military Convergence

The period from 2003 to 2016 was marked by socialist populism, rampant political corruption, and political continuity, starting with the election of President Luis Inácio Lula da Silva (2003–11), known popularly as President Lula, and then the election of his handpicked successor, Dilma Rousseff (2011–16). This period demonstrates the enduring nature of strategic culture elements such as grandeza, because it appealed to both the bureaucratic-military rulers of the 1970s and to the socialist-oriented Workers Party (Partido dos Trabalhadores), the party of Lula and Rousseff. The nationalistic notion of grandeza is undeniably a reoccurring theme in Brazilian strategic culture. Historically used by the military and by the diplomats, now it was also embraced by populist leaders belonging to the opposite side of the political spectrum of the military.

Indeed, by 2005, President Lula rediscovered the political value and a new use to the notion of grandeza to justify his own ambitious agenda and his political goals. President Lula's grandiose vision of projecting Brazil in the global arena included a plan to obtain a permanent seat on the UN Security Council. His policies boosted the country's participation in UN peacekeeping missions, which was part of a broader strategy to integrate defense and foreign policy. These peacekeeping missions highlighted the impor-

---

tance of a holistic approach in the formulation of new, broader national strategy, which included interrelated sectors, such as the economy, politics, the environment, national productivity, science, and technology.[30]

Consequently, in 2005, Lula determined the creation of the first update of the 1996 *National Defense Policy* (Política de Defesa Nacional).[31] The *National Defense Policy* included a much broader and encompassing list of security and defense goals. In particular, the *National Defense Policy* addressed widespread concerns—from the military and civilians alike, with what was described as "international greed, or covetousness" over the riches of Amazon, as well as the need to systematically provide resources for its protection.[32] There was, however, a vacuum between these political goals and a plan to achieve them. This gap was bridged in 2007 when Lula officially mandated the Ministry of Defense to establish a *National Defense Strategy* (A Estratégia Nacional de Defesa), based on the *National Defense Policy*, which was resumed in 2008.[33]

The main elements of the strategy included the need for new technologies, a space program, nuclear capacity for peaceful purposes, restructuring of the armed forces, modernization of the military, hardware acquisitions, and domestic and bor-

---

[30] Arturo C. Sotomayor, *The Myth of the Democratic Peacekeeper: Civil-Military Relations and the United Nations* (Baltimore, MD: Johns Hopkins University Press, 2013), 84; and Andrew Fishman and Max Manwaring, comp., "Brazil's Security Strategy and Defense Doctrine" (brief, U.S. Army War College, Strategic Studies Institute, 2009), 2.

[31] Jungmann, "Aula Inaugural proferida pelo Ministro de Estado da Defesa," slide 9.

[32] Claudio Alexandre De Almeida Freitas, "A Estratégia Nacional de Defesa no Contexto da Amazônia Brasileira" [The National Defense Strategy in the context of the Brazilian Amazon] (diss. presented to the Escola de Comando e Estado-Maior do Exército, Escola Marechal Castello Branco, Rio de Janeiro, 2011), 37.

[33] Fishman and Manwaring, "Brazil's Security Strategy," 1.

der security.[34] Combined, these interrelated efforts blended to maximize focus and capability in a strategic culture theme: the simultaneous development and defense of the Amazon.

The previous sections presented a chronological sequence of political and historical events related to the Amazon; the following sections will detail how the Amazon was consolidated in Brazilian strategic culture as a central theme and as an intrinsic element, as well detailing the role of the military and diplomats in this process.

Security of the Amazon Region

As the previous sections have demonstrated, key historical factors and important geographical features, such as Brazil's continental size, have played a significant role in how Brazilians shaped their strategic culture. This is highlighted in Brazil's 2013 *Defense White Paper* as the immediate and pressing concern with the size of the Amazon was addressed:

> *Brazil has frontiers with 9 other South American countries and one of France's overseas territories, which represent almost 17 thousand kilometers of shared borders. Approximately two thirds of this total is Amazon border.*[35]

Geography is crucial to Brazil's national identity, and that is the reason the Brazilian Amazon is used in this chapter as a case study, because it brings together all the separate elements of strategic culture.

More than just a part of the nation's identity—geography and politics intersect at all levels. The Brazilian Amazon occupies one-third of the national territory. Consequently, within a geopolitical context, Brazil can be considered an entire subregion of South America, because it is the largest country in the region by area and

---

[34] Fishman and Manwaring, "Brazil's Security Strategy," 1.

[35] *Brazil Defense White Paper: Livro Branco de Defesa Nacional* (Brasilia, Brazil: Governo da Republica Fereativa do Brasil, 2012), 17.

population. Moreover, it is distinct because its primary language is Portuguese instead of Spanish, and within the nation there are many subregional cultures.[36] Brazil's landmass is equal to the continental United States, and its population is the fifth largest in the world. The Ministry of Defense made it clear that the Amazon is the focus of national defense:

> *The Amazon is one of the areas of highest interest to the Ministry of Defense. The Pan Amazon, which is constituted by the entire Amazon forest in South America, consists of approximately 40% of the South American continental area and holds 20% of the world's fresh water reserves. The largest area of the Pan-Amazon belongs to Brazil—around 70%. Brazil defends its unconditional sovereignty over the Brazilian Amazon, which comprises over 4 million square kilometers, shelters all kinds of mineral reserves and the planet's largest biodiversity. Brazil's cooperation with other countries holding territory in the Pan-Amazon is essential for the preservation of this natural treasure.*[37]

Considering the earlier discussion of Brazil's strategic culture identity as a peaceful nation, another element of the nation's strategic culture is oriented toward protecting its most valued repository of resources—the Amazon. Accordingly, the *Defense White Paper* highlights that the Amazon region has an immense mineral wealth and the largest volume of water compared to any other river system on Earth. In addition to the Amazon River, the document reflects concern about the underground water related to the Amazon, primarily the Guarani and Alder do Chão Aquifers.[38] The Amazon basin is shared by other countries, such as Bolivia,

---

[36] Brian W. Blouet and Olwyn M. Blouet, eds., *Latin America and the Caribbean: A Systematic and Regional Survey* (Hoboken, NJ: Wiley, 2010), 345.

[37] Blouet and Blouet, *Latin America and the Caribbean*, 19.

[38] Blouet and Blouet, *Latin America and the Caribbean*, 19.

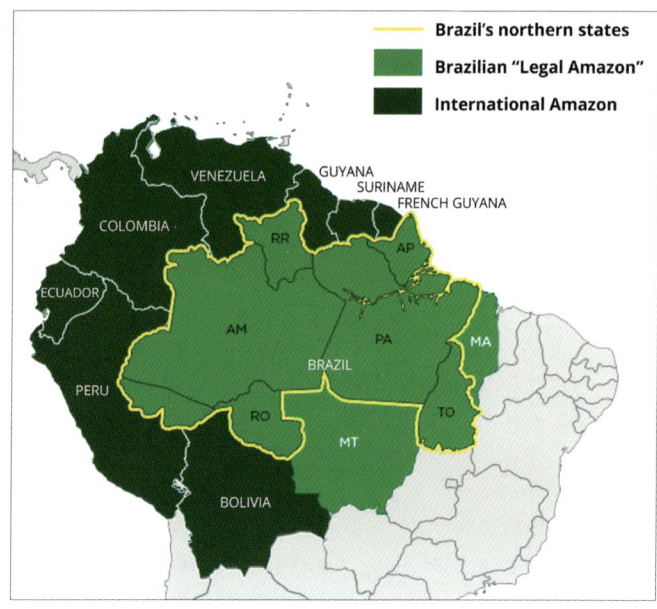

MAP 3

This map illustrates the three Amazon regions referenced in this chapter:
the northern region of Brazil, the Brazilian Legal Amazon,
and the International Amazon.
Portal Paramazonia, adapted by MCU Press

Colombia, Ecuador, Guyana, Peru, Suriname, and Venezuela. The
Amazon River is also strategically important because it has the po-
tential to become a major commercial route into the heart of the
Amazon (map 3).

Brazil's continental dimensions have challenged the country's ability to defend its national sovereignty. Five of Brazil's
nine neighbors are the largest drug-producing countries in
the world. The northern and western borders of the Amazon
rainforest are sparsely populated. Most of Brazil's population
is heavily concentrated on coastal urban areas in the southeast

and northeast regions and the Amazon region is home to only 5.1 percent of Brazil's population.[39]

The Evolution of an Amazonian Strategy

The Brazilian military has always considered the Amazon a primary strategic consideration. For this reason, the Brazilian Army's constitutional mission reflects an internal civil affairs focus. For example, the Brazilian Army's mission statement identifies its role to perform state functions in remote areas of the vast national territory, especially in the Amazon region:

The Army, present in the Amazon since the beginning of the 17th century, has been intensifying its presence by creating new Border Units. Such facilities represent development nuclei around which small urban clusters grow, guaranteeing the national sovereignty in the area. Such pioneering, trail-blazing actions of the Brazilian Army, not only in the Amazon but in other regions throughout the country as well, is part of the Army's constitutional mission. Helping the populating of remote areas, providing a minimum infrastructure until development reaches the area, supplying basic services, this silent work is a solid parcel of the Army's contribution to the progress of the Nation.[40]

Until the 1970s, the Brazilian Army maintained a minimal presence in the Amazon. This began to change during the military regime (1964–85), when the Brazilian military favored economic expansion into the Amazon to promote the integra-

---

[39] "Região Hidrográfica Amazônica" [The Amazonic Hydrographic Region], Agência Nacional de Águas; and "Conheça Cidades e Estados do Brasil" [Learn about the cities and states in Brazil], IBGE [Brazilian Institute of Geography and Statistics—Population of Brazilian Cities], accessed 6 February 2019.

[40] "Amazônia" [The Amazon], Exército Brasileiro [Brazilian Army], accessed 6 February 2019.

tion of remote states, such as Amazonas, Roraima, Acre, and Rondônia. The military regime implemented the National Integration Plan, known as PIN (*Plano de Integração Nacional*) that prioritized Amazonian road construction to foster internal migration to isolated areas: this effort was successful and substantially increased the population of the Amazon until the early 1990s.[41]

The National Integration Plan included a radar project for the Amazon, known as the Radar Mapping Project (*Radar da Amazônia* [RADAM]), an initiative pioneered by the Brazilian government to map the country's natural resources in the Amazon using radar and imaging sensors.[42] Information from RADAM was used to collect data on mineral resources, soil, vegetation, land use, and topography of the Amazon and adjacent areas in the northeast region. The project eventually extended to the rest of the entire national territory. Huge mineral resources were discovered and mapped in the Amazon, which attracted both international and national investments. For example, Carajás Mine, the world's largest iron ore mine, is in the state of Pará in the Amazon region. Carajás also contains valuable natural resources, such as manganese, copper, tin, aluminum, and gold. In the 1970s, U.S. Steel was initially part of a joint venture with the Brazilian government to mine ore, but U.S. Steel withdrew in 1977 by selling its share to the state-owned Companhia Vale do Rio Doce.[43] U.S. Steel originally wanted to mine the ore alone, but the military regime did not allow for a foreign company to have control of a key industry in the heart of the Amazon.

---

[41] "Programa de Integração Nacional (PIN)," [National Integration Program (PIN)] FGV/CPDOC, accessed 7 July 2017.

[42] "RADAM-D," CPRM Servico Geológico do Brasil [Brazil's Geological Service], accessed 5 September 2017.

[43] "RADAM-D"; and "Carajas Iron Ore Mine," Mining Technology, accessed 7 July 2017.

Other military development plans provided for the constructions of large hydroelectric dams in the Amazon.[44] The slogan the military used was "ocupar para não entregar," which translates to "occupy it to avoid surrendering it." The military regime offered tax incentives to foster land use in the Amazon to generate development.[45] At the end of that period, the international community and environmentalists began voicing their concerns over the deforestation of the Amazon. Those claims did not go unnoticed by the military; foreign commercial interests were already under suspicion but now environmentalists were as well. Some environmental groups stoked Brazilian government concerns because they actively promoted antigovernment sentiment. The combination of these factors fueled the fear of direct foreign military intervention in the Amazon.

Security Sensitivities

A summary of these views that demonstrate enduring Brazilian concerns about losing control of the Amazon can be found in an article entitled "Amazonia: Vulnerabilidade—Cobiça—Ameaça" (Amazon: Vulnerability—Covetousness—Threats), published in 2006 and written by General Luiz Eduardo Rocha Paiva.[46] In his article, General Paiva talks about the need to have the armed forces ready to deal with emerging "desafios e novas ameaças" (challenges and new threats), which he identifies as being transnational crime, international terrorism, and loss of authority of the nation-state.[47] General Paiva claims international greed has targeted the Amazon since 1850, when a U.S. naval commander wanted to internationalize the Ama-

---

[44] "The Rights and Wrongs of Belo Monte," *Economist*, 4 May 2013.

[45] Alexei Barrionuevo, "Whose Rain Forest Is This, Anyway?," *New York Times*, 18 May 2008.

[46] Luiz Eduardo Rocha Paiva, "Amazonia: Vulnerabilidade—Cobiça—Ameaça" [Vulnerability—Covetousness—Threats], *Military Review* [Portuguese Edition] (March/April 2008), 5.

[47] Paiva, "Amazonia."

zon River through the implementation of navigation laws that would intrude on Brazilian sovereignty. In 1989, U.S. senator Al Gore commented, "Contrary to what Brazilians think, the Amazon is not their property, it belongs to all of us."[48] In 1989, then-French president François Mitterrand added to the military's list of concerns when he said, "Brazil needs to accept a relative sovereignty over the Amazon."[49] Then in 1992, Mikhail Gorbachev, president of the reform-era Soviet Union (1990–91), declared that Brazil should delegate parts of its rights over the Amazon to a competent international organization, adding fuel to the theory that the international community was orchestrating a way to turn the Amazon into an international zone (i.e., the "internationalization of the Amazon").[50] The historical examples of public figures challenging Brazil's autonomous control over the Amazon are numerous and include historic figures, such as Henry Kissinger and Margaret Thatcher.[51] Collectively these statements seem to form a growing international consensus and confirmed the worst fears of Brazilian civilian and military leadership.

General Paiva identified three actions needed to counter potential foreign intervention in the Amazon: first, there was the need to reduce environmental crimes; second, the need to counter transnational crime by reinforcing border control and air space to neutralize transnational crime and other armed groups that infiltrate the region to confront groups with opposing interests; third, there was the need to revive the policies to integrate the Brazilian indigenous tribes. Paiva also wrote about the lack of resources for the armed forces, citing the fact

---

[48] Paiva, "Amazonia," 3.
[49] Paiva, "Amazonia," 5.
[50] Alexander López, "Environmental Change, Security, and Social Conflicts in the Brazilian Amazon," *Environmental Change & Security Project Report*, no. 5 (Summer 1999): 28.
[51] Paiva, "Amazonia," 4.

that "most equipment used in the Armed Forces are imported," something he claimed was a serious vulnerability because it made "us dependent on someone else to be able to sustain a long-term military operation."[52] This point highlights the general's holistic views, which makes the case for the development of the national defense industry with the strategic purpose of sustaining long-term operations in the Amazon.

The issue of the indigenous people is worth noting because the military was concerned that the Yanomami Park on the Venezuelan-Brazilian border could eventually be turned into an independent indigenous state. In 1989, an activist nongovernmental organization (NGO), Survival International, lobbied the international community for the creation in the northern Amazon of an indigenous reservation in Yanomami Park, which would be the largest indigenous reservation in the world.[53] The military leadership expressed concern, at the time, that the new, independent tribal government that would have resulted from this change could be easily manipulated from abroad, including by NGOs and by the international community.[54]

Unsurprisingly, when the *National Defense Strategy* came out in 2008, many elements of General Paiva's assessment were included in the document. This highlights the fact the Brazilian military has been and continues to be a primary source for Brazilian strategic culture. For instance, the new strategy provided for the armed forces' modernization, increased state presence in the Amazon, and surveillance projects in the Amazon, while giving a boost to the national defense industry by specifically encouraging purchases involving technology trans-

[52] Paiva, "Amazonia," 8.

[53] López, "Environmental Change, Security, and Social Conflicts in the Brazilian Amazon," 2.

[54] López, "Environmental Change, Security, and Social Conflicts in the Brazilian Amazon," 2.

fers over purchases that typically required "buying from over the shelf."[55] This boost to the national defense industry was identified as a need by General Paiva to sustain long-term military conflicts in the region.

Other Security Concerns in the Amazon

Brazil's military leadership saw these statements—from Al Gore's environmental concerns to the NGOs' lobbying for a protected indigenous reservation—as potential security threats to Brazil's sovereignty over the Amazon. These statements brought back fears caused by the long U.S. history of political and military interventions in Latin America, but this time interventionism was under the facade of environmentalism. When General Paiva wrote his 2006 article, he made these fears clear when he referenced the "camouflaged true motives of other opposing actors," regarding the need to control unspecified "illicit transnationals."[56] This veiled reference to the United States might help shed some light on other apparently unrelated events, which resulted on Brazil repositioning more troops to the Amazon.

The drug war long troubled the Brazilian military because it was also regarded as pretext for foreign intervention in the Amazon. The Colombians had been fighting a four-decade long war against the violent insurgency led by the Revolutionary Armed Forces of Colombia (Fuerzas Armadas Revolucionarias de Colombia [FARC]), which had depleted the military resources of the nation and risked the security of the state. This sensitive situation occurred when then-President of Colombia Andrés Pastrana (1998–2002) asked the United States for international support for the creation of Plan Colombia, to

[55] Einaudi, "Brazil and the United States," 6–7.
[56] Paiva, "Amazonia," 7.

assist Colombia with counternarcotic capabilities.[57] While the United States has a history of indirect and direct interference in affairs south of its border, American participation in Plan Colombia (2000–16) specifically sparked new concerns among Brazilian military leaders. Plan Colombia and the suspicions that it created gave the Brazilian military the motivation to redesign its mission.[58] Brazilian concerns about Plan Colombia were ultimately the unstated reason why the Brazilian Army relocated military units from Southern Brazil to the Amazon region. Other incentives existed, such as the Calha Norte Project, which is one of the main military initiatives in the Amazon that will be detailed later, and the Amazon Surveillance System (Sistema de Vigilância da Amazônia [SIVAM])—the air force's satellite surveillance system, that is addressed below.[59]

In fact, the fear of perceived U.S. meddling in the region is another reoccurring theme in Brazilian strategic culture. Dr. Luis Bitencourt, a National Defense University professor and former director of the Brazil Institute at the Woodrow Wilson International Center for Scholars, states that "Brazilians believe that American policymakers tend to exaggerate the relevance of security issues in the region to the detriment of more meaningful themes such as trade and economic development. Brazilians also believe with some reason that in dealing with security issues, Americans resort to the use of force far too soon, in an

---

[57] June S. Beittel, *Colombia: Background, U.S. Relations and Congressional Interest* (Washington, DC: Congressional Research Service, 2012).

[58] Luis Bitencourt, "Security Issues and Challenges to Regional Security, Cooperation: A Brazilian Perspective," in *Perspectives from Argentina, Brazil, and Colombia: Hemispheric Security* (Carlisle, PA: U.S. Army War College, Strategic Studies Institute, 2003), 32; and "Fact Sheet: Peace Colombia—A New Era of Partnership between the United States and Colombia," White House Office of the Press Secretary, 4 February 2016.

[59] Bitencourt, "Security Issues and Challenges to Regional Security, Cooperation," 32.

overwhelming and arrogant manner which may be harmful for negotiated solutions within the region."[60]

Deforestation and Environmental Security

Several decades after the implementation of integration and development projects in the Brazilian Amazon, deforestation continues to be a significant environmental concern in the region, home of the world's largest rainforest. Approximately 20 percent of the forest has been cut down in the past 40 years, with predictions that another 20 percent will be cut in the next 20 years. Despite efforts by the Brazilian government on demarcating forest conservation areas and passing environmental protection legislation, the forest continues to be systematically, though illegally, logged (figure 1). The way forward in dealing with this challenging dilemma is not very clear.[61]

Individuals and groups are unlawfully clearing land for pasture, mining, and logging, while others are pursuing legal activities, such as road building and hydroelectric dam construction, all of which leads to deforestation of the Amazon. For instance, in Northern Brazil, soybean crops are grown mostly on land previously cleared for pasture, but the production of both commodities clearly contribute to make deforestation worse. The soybeans' cycle of production and trade promotes the rapid buildup of transportation infrastructure, such as the construction of roads, barrage systems, and railroads. This buildup in infrastructure also promotes the influx of migrants, attracted to work associated with these activities, resulting in more deforestation.[62]

---

[60] Bitencourt, "Security Issues and Challenges to Regional Security, Cooperation," 21.

[61] Scott Wallace, "Last of the Amazon," *National Geographic*, January 2007; and Blouet and Blouet, *Latin America and the Caribbean*, 381.

[62] Philip M. Fearnside and Adriano M. R. Figueredo, *China's Influence on Deforestation in Brazilian Amazonia: A Growing Force in the State of Mato Grosso* (Boston, MA: Boston University, Global Economic Governance Initiative, 2015), 8.

FIGURE 1
Illegal logging in the state of Para, 2016.
Diretoria de Proteção Ambiental—IBAMA

Antonio Donato Nobre, a renowned researcher at the National Institute for Space Research (Instituto Nacional de Pesquisas Espaciais [INPE]), warns that the logging and burning of the Amazon forest could be connected to worsening droughts in other regions of Brazil. His observations are focused particularly on the 2012–15 drought that affected the whole country—particularly São Paulo, in the state of São Paulo, and the largest city in Latin America, with 30 million people in its metropolitan area. Nobre also forecasts that these interrelated phenomena are likely to eventually lead to more extreme weather events in the southeast region of Brazil.[63]

Nobre's scientific conclusions were based on some 200 studies that tracked the South American rain clouds. He relat-

---

[63] Jonathan Watts, "Brazil's Worst Drought in History Prompts Protests and Blackouts," *Guardian*, 23 January 2015.

ed his findings in a report presented at the United Nations Climate Change Conference in Lima, Peru, in December 2014. These studies pointed out that the devastation of the Amazon is responsible for many aspects of the changes that have recently taken place in the regional climate in the South American continent. The altering of the moisture-generating rain mechanism is caused by the deforestation of the Amazon rainforest. The deforestation, in turn, is a result of illegal logging, mining, farming, and ranching. Nobre explains that

> the Amazon pumps into the atmosphere the humidity that will be transformed into rain in the Midwest, Southeast and Southern regions of Brazil. The larger the deforestation, the less humidity in the atmosphere and therefore less rain. Without the rain, the reservoirs are empty, and the taps dry.[64]

Environmental Laws and Reality

The Brazilian constitution explicitly states the Brazilian people's right to an "ecologically balanced environment" and empowers the government to provide environmental preservation. Deforestation concerns are mentioned in the *Brazil Defense White Paper* in terms of defense, as follows: "The environmental theme is of growing strategic concern for Brazil and brings new challenges for the country in the field of defense. The protection of natural resources is a highlight of the *National Defense Strategy*, mainly regarding the Amazon region."[65] Diplomatically, Brazil cooperates with other countries in the region for the preservation of the Amazon. Brazil is part of the Permanent Secretariat/Amazon Cooperation Treaty Organization (PS/ACTO), and their 2010 *Amazonian Strategic Cooperation*

---

[64] *Falta D'Água Em Cidades Tem a Ver Com a Devastação da Amazônia* [Water shortage in cities has to do with the devastation of the Amazon] (São José dos Campos, Brazil: Instituto Nacional de Pesquisas Espaciais, 2014), 1.
[65] *Brazil Defense White Paper*, 50.

Agenda reflects their common goals, encompassing a series of cooperation initiatives in the field of preservation. Additionally, Brazil is also active in the United Nations Forum on Forests, which strengthens international cooperation for sustainable development and preservation.[66]

Despite the laws in place and Brazil's participation in multilateral forums regarding conservation, some policies being applied in the Amazon may have contradictory goals. This is because some of them are designed to accelerate development of the Amazon while others aim to conserve the environment. Additionally, many conservation policies remain on paper, as they are never enforced because of a lack of funds or a failure to implement them.[67]

Deforestation and Internal Threats: Political and Economic Pressures

There are multiple political and economic factors that interrelate, contributing to an upsurge of deforestation at particular times. As an example, when soybean prices are high and in strong demand in the international market, there is more economic incentive to increase soybean production. This results in more illegal activities and in political pressure to ease environmental laws, which means more deforestation. One of the world's leading scientists in the Amazon, Dr. Philip M. Fearnside of the National Institute for Amazonian Research (Instituto Nacional de Pesquisas da Amazônia [INPA]), explains that deforestation rates in the Brazilian Amazon declined in 2004, coinciding with a decline in soybean demand, which eventually culminated in the 2008 world financial crisis. The reality is that the main driver of lower deforestation rates in that period

---

[66] *Amazonian Strategic Cooperation Agenda* (Brasilia, Brazil: ACTO, 2010).

[67] Xavier Arnauld de Sartre et al., "Eco-Frontier and Place-Making: The Unexpected Transformation of a Sustainable Settlement Project in the Amazon," *Geopolitics* 17, no. 3 (July 2012): 585, http://doi.org/10.1080/14650045.2011.631199.

was the drop in the soybean and beef prices in the international market. There is a direct correlation between less pressure for land clearing to produce soybeans and less deforestation and economic decline. This was exactly what happened during the time when the international prices of soybean and beef dropped in 2004–6—during a low exchange rate for the Brazilian currency—coupled with the lack of profits for exporters at that time. Despite commodity price increases between 2008 and 2012, the exchange rate rise needed to benefit exporters only recovered in 2012. Therefore, once higher international market prices for soybean and beef increased, the pressure to clear land for building infrastructure to transport the soybean has significantly increased again in recent years, reinforcing the correlation between economic activity and deforestation and land clearing.[68]

The combination of the factors mentioned above help explain the Brazilian government's shift from conservation initiatives to a new drive in fostering the development of the Amazon, which in this case means increased deforestation. These recent shifts in Amazon policy is the result of the powerful influence of the *ruralistas* lobby, which are influential and large soybean agribusiness groups who strongly pressure Brazil's National Congress.[69]

The ruralistas helped elect politicians who are pro-business instead of pro-conservation candidates. Their success has had direct and pernicious effects on environmental policies pursued by the congress. An example of the power of the pro-business ruralistas lobby was the federal government's enactment of new laws and regulations in the 2012 Forest Code, which clashed with the 1988 constitution's environmental clauses. Fearnside explains that the new Forest Code, enacted by the government

[68] *Falta D'Água Em Cidades Tem a Ver Com a Devastação da Amazônia*, 10, 16, 21.
[69] Richard Schiffman, "What Lies Behind the Recent Surge of Amazon Deforestation," YaleEnvironment360, 9 March 2015.

in 2012, "weakens critical environmental laws and also offers an amnesty for all those who violated environmental laws before 2008." Basically, he points out, "if you cleared illegally, you got away with it. And the expectation is that if you clear illegally now, sooner or later there will be another amnesty that will forgive your past crimes. On the other hand, if you actually obeyed the law, you lost money. So, the incentives are very perverse."[70] In other words, the Brazilian government provided incentives and amnesty to ignore their own constitution, which was designed to protect the Amazon.

Countering Deforestation: More Internal Threats and Corruption

The Brazilian government implemented a satellite program to monitor deforestation in 1988, a project called Satellite Monitoring of the Brazilian Amazon Forest (*Programa de Monitoramento da Floresta Amazônica Brasileira por Satélite* [PRODES]). The project puts out yearly estimates on deforestation based on images provided by a 220 Landsat/CBER satellite, with all data made available in the internet.[71] The data reported by PRODES includes only "low-cut" deforestation, which are areas that are completely deforested or that have been totally cleared.[72] For instance, the official 2015 PRODES estimate of low-cut deforestation in the Brazilian Amazon is 5,381 square kilometers (2,077 square miles). Between 1988 and 2015, the total deforestation registered was 413,506 square kilometers (159,655 square miles). Antonio Nobre of INPE points out that these official numbers demonstrate that "over the past 40 years, nearly 20 percent of the Amazon has been destroyed; an

---

[70] Schiffman, "What Lies Behind the Recent Surge of Amazon Deforestation."

[71] CBERS is the China-Brazil Earth Resources Satellite.

[72] "Monitoramento de Floresta Amazônica Por Satélite" [Monitoring of the Brazilian Amazon forest by satellite] (presentation, São José dos Campos, Brazil, OBT/INPE, n.d.), 2, accessed 7 July 2017.

area twice the size of Germany; while an additional 22 percent has been seriously compromised."[73] These results were unsettling but clearly not unexpected since the Brazilian government put this project into place as one of the measures to help protect the Amazon. These numbers highlight the magnitude of the task and the need for resources, which were described in the 2008 *National Defense Strategy*, especially the need for the armed forces modernization, increased state presence in the Amazon, and surveillance projects in the Amazon.

Since the inception of PRODES and later by a more accurate and sophisticated surveillance system, known as SIVAM, forest clearing diminished considerably. By 2014, despite the efforts to protect the Amazon, deforestation has significantly increased in response to the renewed lobbying of the ruralistas. Their influence resulted in the passing of a 2012 lax Forest Code and the subsequent detrimental effects in the environment.[74] Indeed, PRODES 2014 data revealed a 190 percent surge in deforestation from August and September of that year.[75] Conservationists took notice of this sudden trend, which meant another uphill political battle was on the way.

Undoubtedly, corruption played a significant role in recent deforestation. At the time, Brazilian scholars understood the problem and were trying to expose government corruption. From inside INPA, Dr. Fearnside denounced this upward trend in deforestation, claiming that "the government hid these

---

[73] *Taxa Estimada do Desmatamento da Amazônia Legal Para Período Ago/2014– Jul/2015* [Estimated rate of deforestation of the legal Amazon for the period of August 2014 to July 2015] (Brasilia, Brazil: Ministério da Ciência, Tecnologia e Inovação, 2015), 5, 10; and Reed Johnson and Rogerio Jelmayer, "Deforestation Sparks Brazilian Debate," *Wall Street Journal,* 4 December 2014.

[74] President Dilma Rousseff's first term was from 2011 to 2014; her second term began 2 January 2015. She was impeached and removed from office on 31 August 2016.

[75] Jonathan Watts, "Amazon Rainforest Losing Ability to Regulate Climate, Scientist Warns," *Guardian*, 31 October 2014.

figures before the [2014 presidential] election."[76] These claims are no longer speculation or opinions; they are now historical facts and a component of the Brazilian political scandal that helped bring down President Dilma Rousseff. Her government manipulated other important numbers in the federal budget and committed fiscal fraud—the main legal accusation that led to her impeachment from the presidency in 2016. This fraudulent accounting used by Rousseff's government paid off in the short term, allowing her to win a second term in a close 2014 race. Despite the success of Rousseff's reelection, Fearnside denounced the delay of the publication of data, which revealed the dramatic increase in deforestation. Thus, the Amazon's security is also threatened by internal factors, such as corruption and unsustainable economic practices.[77]

Interweaving Security Sensitivities into the National Defense Strategy

As stated previously, the Amazon has historically been a major focus of the Brazilian military's strategic thinking, actions, and resources. However, due to the difficulties of effectively policing such an immense swath of territory, this eventually led to a lack of state presence in the region, resulting in a structural inability to enforce environmental preservation of the Amazon. As a result, this security gap became an intrinsic part of the Brazilian Army mission authorized by the Brazilian national constitution. The military's view that the Amazon is under the threat of being annexed by the international community became an integral part of the *National Defense Policy* and there-

---

[76] Schiffman, "What Lies Behind the Recent Surge of Amazon Deforestation." The August and September data would normally have been released in October, before the 26 October presidential election, but the government of Dilma Rousseff sat on the data, and it was not disclosed until the end of November.

[77] Joe Leahy, "What Is Brazil's President Dilma Rousseff Accused of?," *Financial Times*, 12 May 2016; and Schiffman, "What Lies Behind the Recent Surge of Amazon Deforestation."

fore the *National Defense Strategy*. Even before the *National Defense Strategy* was published, which was soon after the creation of the Ministry of Defense, the focus of military doctrine was to integrate the various projects in the Amazon.

There is an ever-evolving cause and effect relationship regarding how military strategic culture informs the *National Defense Strategy* and the army's organizational culture. Additionally, the Ministry of Defense has been instrumental in orchestrating the national dialogue by promoting conferences, symposiums, and talks on security concerns with Brazilian society. This is especially true in relation to topics on the Brazilian Amazon. Other strategic culture topics that are discussed within Brazilian society include the concept of the Blue Amazon (i.e., Brazilian offshore natural resources, which the Brazilian Navy calls "Amazônia Azul") oil reserves in deep waters, cyberspace, and borders to a lesser extent.[78]

It was, therefore, a widely accepted view in the country that the Amazon is vulnerable, and that multiple threats seriously jeopardized national sovereignty. For most Brazilians— civilians and military alike—the Amazon region evokes unified concern from a security standpoint. In fact, the Amazon may be the only topic that arouses a collective and emotional response from both Brazilian leadership and the general population; most Brazilians generally perceive outside concerns regarding the Amazon's ecosystem as an attempt to appropriate untapped resources, which evokes highly emotional and nationalistic reactions.[79]

---

[78] Reinaldo Sótão Calderaro, "A Ação do Ministério da Defesa na Articulação da Política de Defesa com A Política Externa Brasileira a Partir de 2007" [Defense Ministry actions in the articulation of defense policy with Brazilian foreign policy after 2007] (diss. presented to the Escola De Comando e Estado-Maior do Exército, Escola Marechal Castello Branco, 2013), 120.

[79] Bitencourt, "Security Issues and Challenges to Regional Security, Cooperation," 21.

While the national government attempts to reconcile competing priorities between their environmental concern for the Amazon and the more pressing need to appease their political base, the army and the MOD remain firmly focused on the security of the Amazon. The MOD's organizational structure highlights the importance of the Amazon, with the Center for the Management and Operation of the Amazon Protection System (*Centro Gestor e Operacional do Sistema de Proteção da Amazônia* [CENSIPAM]) representing one of the four policy pillars under MOD's secretary general. CENSIPAM's policies rely on a partnership between federal and state organizations, as well as NGOs, to promote a gradual activation of the Amazon Protection System (*Sistema de Proteção da Amazônia* [SIPAM]).[80]

The 2005 *National Defense Policy* also encompassed the *Military Defense Policy*, with specific guidelines to Brazil's Joint Command and Staff of the armed forces regarding military strategies. Therefore, following the publication of these guidelines, the *2006 Military Defense Strategy* directed the publication of operational plans. In 2007, *Military Defense Doctrine* established the operational guidance to enable the armed forces to execute missions as allowed in the constitution.[81] From the linkages described above, one can see how strategic culture elements, particularly regarding the Amazon region and its importance to the concept of Brazilian strategic culture, informed the *National Defense Strategy* and how these elements trickled down, affecting the organizational culture of the armed forces.

Additionally, Brazilian Army doctrine is constantly updated and refined by the army's Command and Staff College (*Escola de Comando do Estado-Maior do Exército* [ECEME]) and by the War School (*Escola Superior de Guerra* [ESG]), which

---

[80] *Brazil Defense White Paper*, 58, 64.
[81] Freitas, *A Estratégia Nacional de Defesa no Contexto da Amazônia Brasileira*, 38.

are both directly linked to the Ministry of Defense. ESG is also an institute of advanced studies and research in the areas of national development, security, and defense. There has been intense collaboration and coordination between ESG and the diplomatic corps in a process that has intensified between the 1950s and the 1970s. Collaboration culminated in the 1990s, as the diplomats and the military authored the *National Defense Policy* and updated the national defense strategies of 2005, 2008, 2012, and 2016, including the *Brazil Defense White Paper*, published in 2012.[82]

The Brazilian Army and the other branches of the armed forces contribute to the Institute for Joint Operations Doctrine, with papers, dissertations, theses related to national defense, and strategies. All these combined efforts assist in the formulation of specific priorities from national defense to doctrine level, which includes the strategic culture elements that make their way into the *National Defense Strategy* and are brought back down in the form of updated doctrines. For example, the new armed forces doctrine has been integrated with the *National Defense Strategy*, aligning the armed forces operational capacity throughout the national territory. There are new elements of strategic culture, specifically originally related to the Amazon that were expanded to include the entire national territory, which are now clearly present in the doctrine. These concepts were summarized in two main strategic concepts in the doctrine: *dissuasion* and *presence*. *Dissuasion* refers to the need to maintain sufficiently strong forces for immediate action, including military presence in the entire national territory to guarantee constitutional law and order, sovereignty, national

---

[82] *Brazil Defense White Paper*, 65; and Jungmann, "Aula Inaugural proferida pelo Ministro de Estado da Defesa," slides 8–9.

integration, and development.[83] In other words, the military succeeded in affecting national policy, adapting doctrine, and in attaining additional forces, as they perceived they needed. This process reinforces their role as the keepers and primary policy makers of Brazilian strategic culture.

In addition to these concerted efforts, the *National Defense Strategy* provided for other complementary strategic actions in the Brazilian armed forces. With the *2008 National Defense Strategy* in place, the Brazilian Army developed several new interrelated projects in the Amazon region to align their mission to safeguard national sovereignty with other sensitive scientific initiatives prescribed in the *National Strategy on Science, Technology and Innovation*. Pro-Amazon (*Proamazônia*) is one such project, created to promote the expansion of research and the use of new technologies in the Amazon. The ultimate objective is "to promote sustainable development in the nation's most strategic region."[84] Another objective of the project is to align other command and control projects of the Brazilian army in the Amazon with Proamazônia.

Proamazônia's goals include having the Brazilian Army provide logistical support for several ongoing projects that are the responsibility of other governmental agencies and various academic institutions. For example, there are projects from the University of Rio de Janeiro; University of São Paulo; INPA; SIPAM, which was created to manage the actions implemented by SIVAM; the Brazilian Agricultural Research Corporation (*Empresa Brasileira de Pesquisa Agropecuária* [EMBRAPA]); and

---

[83] Carlos Roberto Resende et al., "O Exército Brasileiro e a Gestão Ambiental da Amazônia no Século XXI: Uma Visão Estratégica" [The Brazilian Army and the environmental management of the Amazon in the twenty-first century: A strategic vision] (paper presented at the Brazilian Army Management School, 2004); and Freitas, *A Estratégia Nacional de Defesa no Contexto da Amazônia Brasileira*, 23.

[84] "Amazônia 'Conhecer para Proteger' " ["Amazon 'know it to protect it' "] Exercito Brasileiro Comando Militar da Amazonia [Brazilian Army Military Command of the Amazon], accessed 28 February 2018.

others.[85] These various projects include assisting the Yanomami indigenous people, researching programs in biodiversity in the western portion of the Amazon, protecting wildlife with preservation programs, and funding water-quality projects and geopolitical projects.

In sum, the Brazilian Army has implemented dozens of coordinated projects, actions, and plans in the Amazon to align with the *National Defense Strategy*. The way these projects interrelate and derive from the major defense document on the land, informing doctrine down to the daily job of an army unit, were detailed in a very informative study by Major Claudio Freitas. His 2011 dissertation for ECEME titled "The *National Defense Strategy* in the Context of the Brazilian Amazon" provided an in-depth account of the process.[86] He explains how all these combined new actions and directives, also originally envisioned for the Amazon, but later expanded to the whole territory, fomented continual internal organizational adaptations and changes. One such action included the implementation in 2009 of the Strong Arm Strategy (*Estratégia Braço Forte*), which involved two levels—an articulation level and an equipment level, with the combined goal to modernize the army.[87] The Articulation Plan included the Protected Amazon Plan (*Programas Amazônia Protegida*) and the Nation's Sentinel (*Sentinela da Pátria*), with the first consisting of projects to strengthen the land-based military presence in the Amazon region and the second including projects to reorganize and adapt operational and logistical structures in the military commands

---

[85] *Forests Sourcebook: Practical Guidance for Sustaining Forests in Development Cooperation* (Washington, DC: International Bank for Reconstruction and Development, World Bank, 2008), 251.

[86] Freitas, *A Estratégia Nacional de Defesa no Contexto da Amazônia Brasileira*, 22.

[87] Freitas, *A Estratégia Nacional de Defesa no Contexto da Amazônia Brasileira*, 22.

in the area.[88] The plan for equipment renewal included a program for mobility and a program to equip the force, based on a vision for the future of the army that takes into account the evolution of military doctrine, science, and technology.

Other Strategic Projects in the Amazon

As prescribed in the *National Defense Strategy*, by 2004, Project Calha Norte became the centerpiece of Brazil's comprehensive strategy for sustainable development of the Amazon region. The fully operational project prioritized settlement and infrastructure construction, as well as the creation of special border platoons along the northern border in the Amazon region. The project was equipped with an operational system for the surveillance of Amazonia—SIVAM—consisting of radar and environmental sensors. SIVAM provides tools to monitor problems in the Brazilian Amazon, such as illegal mining, drug trafficking, forest burning, agrarian conflicts, invasion of indigenous lands, and cattle ranching. Brazil's experience with SIVAM is considered an example of extensive cooperation and technology sharing between Brazil and the United States.[89]

In addition to Project Calha Norte, the Ministry of Defense has secured resources for many other projects in the coming years, "especially for projects that involve air space, cybernetics, and nuclear power, such as Prosub, Sisfron, KC 390, Proteger and the army's Cybernetics Center."[90] The Integrated Border Monitoring System (*Sistema Integrado de Monitoramento de Fronteiras* [SISFRON]) will allow the land forces to monitor

---

[88] Freitas, *A Estratégia Nacional de Defesa no Contexto da Amazônia Brasileira*, 22.

[89] John A. Cope and Andrew Parks, *Frontier Security: The Case of Brazil* (Washington, DC: National Defense University Press, 2016), 1; "Raytheon Presentation: SIVAM Presentation on Nov. 13th, 2002," MIT, 13 November 2002; and Julia E. Sweig, "NSA, SIVAM, Dilma and Barack," *Folha de São Paulo*, 17 July 2013.

[90] Calderaro, "A Ação do Ministério da Defesa na Articulação da Política de Defesa com A Política Externa Brasileira a Partir de 2007," 120.

national borders and to promptly respond to any aggression or threat, especially in the Amazon region.[91]

In 2011, the government launched another security initiative, the Strategic Borders Plan, which provided for military and law enforcement security operations to counter criminal activities. The plan also aligned with the military's wish list that was included in the *2008 National Strategy of Defense*. Accordingly, the National Congress of Brazil granted the armed forces policing powers within 90 miles of the frontier, which included provisions to better integrate actions with police operations.[92] This meant that all three branches of the armed forces would be restructured to better monitor and control the border, allowing for improved mid- and long-range capabilities. The plan's implementation has yielded improvements in counternarcotic operations as well as illegal weapons and various illegal commodities' interdiction.

Since the publication of the *2008 National Defense Strategy*, the armed forces have a clear mandate to protect the resources of the Brazilian Amazon. The strategy provided the armed forces with provisions and increased financial support to allow for its current modernization and restructuring. This includes the incorporation of sophisticated technology to increase the armed forces' presence in the Amazon region, as well as incentives to boost the Brazilian defense sector with the development of new equipment, which includes favoring purchases of defense equipment involving technology transfer and giving preference to the Brazilian defense industry instead of imports.

Conclusion

Because the armed forces represent one of the main developers

[91] *Brazil Defense White Paper*, 74.
[92] Cope and Parks, "Frontier Security," 12.

of Brazilian strategic culture, the need to secure the Brazilian Amazon will therefore remain the centerpiece of Brazilian strategic culture for decades to come. Despite all the initiatives, policies, and actions taken, new potential security risks continue to emerge in the region, forcing the army and government to deal with both the perceived security threats and with the ever-growing security challenges that currently exist in the Amazon. These new security challenges branch off into political pressures, socioeconomic problems, and environmental risks that gradually accumulate each day in the Amazon region. The current state of disarray in Venezuela adds to the list of security concerns, which will likely spill over to the Brazilian side if civil war breaks out in that country. At the same time, there is new evidence of risks posed by deforestation of the Amazon, which will impact water scarcity in the rest of the country. Water scarcity in the southeast region and elsewhere in the country is likely to increase and will slowly put pressure on the Brazilian military to increase their control of the Amazon region.

Gradually, the armed forces might concede that their original fears that the international community wants to control the Amazon might give way to an even more challenging problem—preventing corruption. As the military realizes that the main enemy of the integrity of the Brazilian Amazon is political corruption, they might feel compelled to counter it more boldly. For instance, the armed forces may feel pressured to increase their ability to conduct police actions in the region. This would promote a shift toward providing internal stability, which is the opposite direction of what the politicians have been attempting to establish since the creation of the Ministry of Defense in 1999. Those new missions may need to include concerted and well-funded domestic actions to counter corruption and, subsequently, the deforestation that comes with it. The need to protect the Amazon from deforestation will encounter problems as well and will most likely clash with economic pressures to maintain strong momentum for exports of commodities to generate hard currency for the country, something that soybeans and beef generate.

The correlations between security and environmental responsibility might take time to consolidate in military doctrine and in the national narrative. The wealthier southern Brazilian states will eventually put more pressure on their political representatives to counter deforestation in the Amazon. These states are responsible for most of Brazil's national industrial output and are heavily dependent on hydroelectricity. Recent and unprecedented droughts are possibly also aggravated by deforestation in the Amazon, along with various climate-related reasons, such as pollution of riverbeds and destruction of ciliary forests, which are forests along basins and springs that provide protection to the river. This will encourage all of society to regard the destruction of the Amazon as a threat to the nation's economy, directly affecting a large segment of the population's lives and livelihood, as well as impacting Brazil's gross domestic product.

The armed forces will continue to adapt their doctrine and their organizational culture to these new challenges, as the Amazon will become an increasingly sensitive topic in bilateral relations with the United States. These sensitivities will trickle down to the agency level that engage in security cooperation, trade, development of nuclear energy, or climate change related forums. This means that U.S. officials, military or civilian, that deal with the Brazilian military will need to be aware of the high value that the Brazilian military and population place on the autonomy of the Amazonian territory within its national boundaries. The Amazon is indeed a topic that could evoke nationalistic, emotional responses from the Brazilian government, government officials, the military, and civilians alike.

CHAPTER
5

A NEW STATE WITH A NASCENT STRATEGIC CULTURE

International and Domestic Influences in Kosovo

by George Bogden, PhD

Introduction

The western end of the main boulevard in Kosovo's capital, Pristina, embodies the dichotomies and contradictions that shape the country's strategic culture. Facing the square in front of the parliament, to the left, a statue of Skanderbeg dominates one's field of vision. He was a mighty medieval warlord who turned against the Ottoman empire to lead Albanian Christians in armed resistance against Muslim rule. His horse is midstride, his sword unsheathed. On the opposite side of the square stands Ibrahim Rugova, the man considered the nation's first president. A literary as well as political figure, he was an ardent supporter of nonviolence and perpetually campaigned for Kosovo's independence among the international community, which earned him the sobriquet "Gandhi of the Balkans." In these two images, the Kosovar will for self-determination, deeply embedded nationalism, capacity for marshal resistance, and reliance on international support and intervention are woven together, leaving the thoughtful observer with an uneasy sense of paradox.

To search for Kosovo's strategic culture is to address myths and aspirations, not only of its population but also those harbored by the world leaders who shouldered the effort to bring the country into existence. Having just celebrated its first decade of independence, now is an appropriate time to reflect on key strategic ideas that underlie realities on the ground, and that are reflected in Kosovo's security and military institutions. Though still in their infancy, these organs of the state bear discernible attributes worthy of scrutiny by students seeking to understand how a nascent country develops a defining perspective on military affairs.

Given the typical scope of case studies in this text, one might think it is futile to attempt to decipher the strategic culture of a small, new country such as Kosovo, with a population of less than two million. The government in Pristina is still attempting to achieve broad recognition as a state, to consolidate its legitimacy, and to establish basic functions of governance, which it continues to share with the United Nations Mission in Kosovo (UNMIK). Yet, several features of Europe's youngest democracy make it a prime candidate for examination as a case study in strategic culture. First and foremost, it serves as a contemporary example of how a post-conflict society responds to the pressures to change from within as well as those exerted by outside forces. Kosovo has struggled and will continue to act to transform its military capacities. The efforts and resources used to rid itself of a former government perceived as illegitimate are being redirected into the competencies necessary for institutionalized self-defense.

Prelude to Independence

Any analysis of Kosovo's strategic culture must begin with a brief reprise of the political circumstances that led to its existence. The topic of this chapter, the strategic culture of one state, is too narrow to contend with even a cross-section of the history of the entire Balkan region. To deal seriously with the whole peninsula's rich past is to confront the legacies of multiple empires—Greek, Achaemenid, Roman, Byzantine, Venetian, Ottoman, and Austro-Hungarian, to name but a few. It would also require a reckoning of the interplay of many ethnic and religious dimensions of identity—among them Albanian, Serbian, Bosnian, Croatian, as well as Catholic and Orthodox Christian, not to mention the Islamic faith. For millennia, Balkan peoples have governed themselves and been governed through a shifting mosaic of power and cultural influence, accepting and overturning numerous systems of rule and ideological attachments. Kosovo, as a small territory in the region, has remained enveloped in these crosscurrents, reflecting the complex distinctions its populations have drawn to define and redefine their relationships to neighboring political entities. Rather than providing a complete account of this remarkable history, it is useful and appropriate to examine the position of Kosovo in the twentieth century. This review should proceed by paying special attention to the two decades, beginning in 1997, in which it began on its current course toward development as a state.

Although the history of territorial disputes in the Balkans remains highly contested, the broad outlines of Kosovo's political position in the last century are clear. The borders of what is known today as the Republic of Kosovo were roughly drawn within the Socialist Federal Republic of Yugoslavia in 1946. At that time, it was first recognized as an administrative unit of the constituent Socialist Republic of Serbia, itself part of a larger Yugoslavian polity.[1] Like the dynamics leading to fragmentation elsewhere in the region in the 1990s, Kosovo's struggle for self-determination began in earnest in the 1960s. Although

---

[1] Miranda Vickers, *Between Serb and Albanian: A History of Kosovo* (New York: Columbia University Press, 1998), 223–24.

interethnic tensions flared in the region throughout the twentieth century, they became particularly intense with the reversal of the decentralization of authority that occurred in Yugoslavia in the 1960s. After this process culminated with the ratification of the 1974 Constitution, authorities in the States Councils of Yugoslavia began to roll back provisions for autonomy in certain provinces, such as Kosovo. Its special status as the Socialist Autonomous Province of Kosovo within Yugoslavia's complex system of governance coincided with demographic changes and fluctuations in nationalist sentiments, which pitted a majority of ethnic Albanians, most of whom were Sunni Muslims, against other ethnic and religious groups, especially ethnic Serb Orthodox Christians.

Throughout the 1980s, the government in Belgrade began to answer claims of oppression made by Serbs residing in Kosovo. Leaders in the Serbian minority community melded their grievances with claims about the special meaning ascribed to Kosovo in Serbian history. They highlighted the cultural significance of battles fought in the area and the spiritual importance of certain churches and monasteries.[2] These trends reached their first crescendo when, on 28 June 1989, President Slobodan Milošević addressed a crowd of ethnic Serbs in Gazimestan. He ostensibly sought to commemorate the sixth centennial anniversary of the Battle of Kosovo. Yet, he was also simultaneously signaling changes in Belgrade's priorities to Serbs throughout the Balkans. Shortly afterward, he began a campaign of fear and political pressure to achieve his two primary goals for governing Kosovo. At the time, the president of Serbia sought to persuade central Yugoslav authorities to lessen Kosovo's autonomy, while reshaping local institutions to en-

---

[2] Noel Malcolm, *Kosovo: A Short History* (New York: New York University Press, 1998), 195–96.

gage in multifaceted forms of oppression of ethnic Albanians.[3] The systematic revocation of previous political concessions to Albanian leaders in the region underlaid this change. Measures included banning the Albanian language in public primary and secondary schools. Kosovar Albanians who lived through the period commonly characterize these policies as constituting a form of "apartheid."[4]

In response, a long-standing, nonviolent movement for independence began among Kosovar Albanians in the 1990s. Although an initial attempt to attain sovereignty occurred in 1992, it failed to gain recognition by any other state than Albania. The question of Kosovo's independence was left largely unanswered by the international agreements that ended major conflicts elsewhere in the Balkans.[5] Although the first phase of the dissolution of the former Yugoslavia—which ended with the 1995 Dayton Accords—did not resolve the tensions surrounding Kosovo's governance, they did demonstrate to an aggrieved Albanian ethnic majority that the international community could and would intervene in the Balkans. The last credible census that took place in Kosovo before the conflicts of the 1990s occurred in 1981. Ethnic Albanians represented 77 percent of the population, with Serbs constituting 13

---

[3] From the period, see the "What's Next for Slobodan Milošević?," *Economist*, 5 June 1999, 24. For a broader analysis of this turning point, see Carole Rogel, "Kosovo: Where It All Began," *International Journal of Politics, Culture, and Society* 17, no. 1 (Fall 2003): 167–80, http://doi.org/10.1023/A:1025397128633.

[4] This tendency is mentioned by the historical surveys of the period cited above and was confirmed in the majority of the interviews this researcher conducted. Without prompting, the subjects of these interviews would put forward this characterization and discuss how it influenced the new government's policies and disposition toward Serbia.

[5] The Kosovo Memory Book database, Humanitarian Law Center, continually updated, accessed online for the last time on 7 July 2016.

percent.[6] In 1991, the Federal Statistical Office of the Federal Republic of Yugoslavia estimated that of a population totaling approximately 1,956,000 in 1991, 82 percent were Albanians, 10 percent Serbs, and 8 percent others.[7] The formidable ethnic Albanian community remained deeply unsatisfied with worsening rule by Belgrade.

With regard to Kosovo's development of strategic culture, the late 1990s constituted a crucial period. Kosovo's ensuing war of liberation defined its orientation to surrounding populations and to its regional environment. The conflagration resulted in independence. And out of the conflict came both the basic institutions of Kosovo's defense forces, as well as the international framework that still applies to some aspects of its governance.

By 1996, local Albanian populations became sympathetic to calls for a violent mode of opposition to Serbian rule, conducted by the Kosovo Liberation Army (KLA). Armed resistance persisted through the late 1990s, answered by increasingly brutal responses from Serbian security forces. Early massacres are too numerous to count. Cases like the Serbian attack on the village of Prekaz came to symbolize the asymmetry between Albanian militants, who commanded small bands of irregular soldiers, and the organized, state-funded security forces sent by Belgrade to quell the rapidly growing rebellion. The martyrdom of Adem Jashari—killed after a siege of his home in Prekaz following multiple violent confrontations with a so-called antiterrorism unit—exhibited the unequal contest between Albanian forces and their foes, as well as the fierceness

---

[6] The official 1991 Yugoslav census was largely boycotted by the ethnic Albanians. This is noted in Janusz Bugajski, *Political Parties of Eastern Europe: A Guide to Politics in the Post-Communist Era* (New York: M. E. Sharpe, 2002), 479.

[7] *Statistical Yearbook of Yugoslavia* (Belgrade: Federal Statistical Office, Government of the Federal Republic of Yugoslavia, 1997).

of Belgrade's methods to achieve military objectives.[8] Jashari, often depicted holding an automatic rifle, is memorialized as the father of the KLA, illustrating the continued presence of early guerrilla fighters in the imagination of the national community. That his death is commemorated throughout urban landscapes, as well as in popular art, literature, and musical lyrics, conveys the common understanding that Kosovo's struggle has not yet ended. This narrative's message is clear: it is the duty of free Kosovar peoples to resist injustice until the bitter end.

After the collapse of a cease-fire orchestrated by the United States in 1998, a multilateral conference was convened in 1999, resulting in the Rambouillet Accords. This agreement required greater autonomy for Kosovo.[9] Once Serbia rejected its terms, a bombing campaign commenced, through which the North Atlantic Treaty Organization (NATO) sought to compel Milošević to withdraw all armed military units from Kosovo. Open war raged between Albanian militias under the direction of the KLA and Serbian forces. Although statistics about casualties from the conflict are still occasionally revised, the most commonly cited figures are from the Humanitarian Law Center.[10] It suggests that 13,517 persons were killed during the armed conflict in Kosovo. Approximately 1,886 persons remain missing, and discoveries as late as 2013 of mass graves with hundreds of Albanian bodies suggested the final death count will continue to rise.[11] Human rights violations by

---

[8] Heike Krieger, ed., *The Kosovo Conflict and International Law: An Analytical Documentation 1974–1999* (Cambridge, UK: Cambridge University Press, 2001), 92–96.

[9] Larry Minear et al., *NATO and Humanitarian Action in the Kosovo Crisis*, occasional paper no. 36 (Providence, RI: Thomas J. Watson Jr. Institute for International Studies, Brown University, 2000), 34–35.

[10] For academic rather than political critiques of the death toll count, see Elizabeth Minor, *Towards the Recording of Every Casualty: Analysis and Policy Recommendations from a Study of 40 Casualty Recorders* (London: Oxford Research Group, 2012).

[11] "EULEX: Human remains found in Rudnica," b92, 13 December 2013.

Serbian forces against Albanians during the conflict spanned many aspects of life that have only recently been addressed. The international community's renewed attention to the survivors of sexual violence during the war, and the new national memorial created in Pristina in their memory, is but one example.[12]

Postwar Reform and the KLA's Recrudescence

After years of fighting, Belgrade relented. Milošević's government relinquished direct control of the region shortly after the United Nations Security Council passed Resolution 1244 in June 1999. It created UNMIK to administer transitional authority in the province. Although the resolution set out greater autonomy for Kosovo, authorizing a NATO peacekeeping force to implement these measures, it also reaffirmed the territorial integrity of the Federal Republic of Yugoslavia (Serbia), of which Kosovo legally remained a province. [13] At this stage,

---

[12] For information regarding the belated international response to the legacy of sexual violence during Kosovo's war of independence, see Siobhan Hobbs, *Designing a Reparation Programme for Victims of Conflict-Related Sexual Violence in Kosovo: Principles, Practices and Recommendations* (New York: UN Women, 2016), 2–6. The 2016 establishment and building of a war memorial in downtown Pristina for these victims, across from the commemorative *Newborn* sculpture, which uses the moniker "Heroines" in Albanian, served as a symbolic commitment to pursuing justice for them in the years to come. While much of the investigation of human rights violations during the decade after the conflict centered on the crimes of the Serbian state and its security forces, atrocities committed by Albanian forces have begun to take a more pronounced position in Kosovo's society and in its relations with the European governments and the United States. See Marija Ristic, "Council Adopts Kosovo Organ Trafficking Resolution," *Balkan Insight*, 25 January 2011, 1–4. See also Marija Ristic, "Serbia Locates Alleged Organ Trafficking Doctor," *Balkan Insight*, 2 September 2014, 2.

[13] On this latter point, UN Security Council Resolution 1244 read, "Reaffirming the commitment of all Member States to the sovereignty and territorial integrity of the Federal Republic of Yugoslavia and the other States of the region, as set out in the Helsinki Final Act." See United Nations Security Council, Resolution 1244 (10 June 1999).

the considerable role of the international community in creating Kosovo's security institutions came into effect.

Resolution 1244 clearly accorded full governmental authority—described as "reserved powers"—to the special representative of the secretary general (SRSG). This individual was tasked with coordinating all aspects of the civilian and military organizations acting to secure Kosovo. The SRSG remained responsible for deciding parameters for the reconstruction of the country and the establishment of its institutions.[14] Although UN authorities influenced, to a significant degree, all aspects of government in post-conflict Kosovo, the most salient to the development of strategic culture was the so-called first pillar of the mission, humanitarian assistance, later renamed justice and security. This particular wing of the UN mission set up two key organs of state: the Kosovo Police Service (KPS) and the Kosovo Protection Corps (KPC). The latter emerged directly from the KLA, and its mandate was initially limited to civil protection and emergency services, confined to addressing the needs of municipalities. The diminution of the scope of the former fighting force's purpose was compounded by the decision of the SRSG to deny local institutions the remit of national defense and intelligence collection. Instead of initially setting up Kosovar institutions to address these areas of policy, the SRSG retained control over these state functions.[15]

As a result, the first half-decade following the end of hostilities in 1999 was marked by the absence of local Kosovar

---

[14] United Nations Security Council, Resolution 1244. In addition, it is worth noting the conclusion of the Independent International Commission on Kosovo with regard to the concept of *reserved powers*. The body argued that, as a result of this mechanism, "instead of the substantial self-government promised the Kosovars under Resolution 1244, they will instead get very limited autonomy." *The Follow-Up to the Kosovo Report: Why Conditional Independence?* (Stockholm: Independent International Commission on Kosovo, 2001), 20.

[15] Florian Qehaja, *International or Local Ownership?: Security Sector Development in Post-Independent Kosovo* (Washington, DC: Westphalia Press, 2017), 55–56.

security actors from the primary institutions that typically play host to a state's strategic culture. UNMIK remained particularly stubborn about the creation of an independent Kosovar defense bureaucracy. UN authorities refused to hand over responsibilities incrementally with regard to national security. The UN mission justified its draconian stance based on a rigid application of UN Security Council Resolution 1244. Steps to amend this policy were never charted, let alone adopted, before specific guidance from UN Headquarters made a gradual transition mandatory.

An intermediate step toward greater integration of local security forces was initiated in 2005. In that year, UNMIK began the formal procedure of an annual *Internal Security Sector Review* (ISSR). This program monitored the operation of security institutions, proposing means of increasing their capacities and producing greater self-sufficiency. Eventually, the ISSR identified goals to be orchestrated by Kosovar leaders. ISSR recommendations were the product of attempted engagement with a broad diversity of civic leaders in Kosovo. Planners accepted advice and guidance from a representative cross-section of urban and rural communities. Nonetheless, the individuals driving the process—conducting interviews and compiling reports always hailed from international organizations.[16] They were inherently removed from the local view of security imperatives on the ground because they were separated by their experience from the outlook of those who lived through the war for independence. Only in its second year did the ISSR begin to recommend greater involvement and further input from conflict survivors, as well as returned members of the diaspora. UNMIK responded by hiring Kosovars more often and design-

---

[16] Florian Qehaja and Mentor Vrajolli, *Context Analysis of Security Sector Reform in Kosovo, 1999–2009* (Pristina: Kosovar Centre for Security Studies, 2011), 14.

ing channels of communication with members of civil society invested in questions of national defense.[17]

Subsequent processes undertaken between 2006 and 2008 deeply impacted Kosovo's strategic culture after formal independence arrived. Intermittent episodes of unrest, punctuated by riots and coinciding with the mass exodus of ethnic Serbs, served as a prelude to contentious negotiations that began in 2006 regarding Kosovo's final status, as had been prescribed by the UN Security Council. The appointment of Martti Ahtisaari as UN special envoy in February 2006, led to a lengthy period of exchange among international stakeholders about how Kosovo would be governed in the future. Leaders in Belgrade and Pristina stridently disagreed about the extent of self-rule that Kosovo should be accorded. The special envoy submitted a "plan" for independence "supervised by the international community" a year after his appointment.[18] This document, which enumerated guiding principles for Kosovo's integration into the international community, aimed to serve as a framework for action by the UN Security Council to fulfill the end goal proposed by the special envoy. Russian opposition ensured that a Security Council resolution implementing the Ahtisaari Plan

---

[17] This reality is reflected in the report, *Internal Security Sector Review (ISSR) in Kosovo* (Pristina: United Nations Development Programme, 2006).

[18] UN Secretary-General Ban Ki-moon, *Report of the Special Envoy of the Secretary-General on Kosovo's Future Status,* S/2007/168 (New York: United Nations Security Council, 26 March 2007), 5.

never passed.[19] Violation of state sovereignty remains the principle objection cited by Moscow's permanent representative to the UN, who has consistently threatened to veto Security Council resolutions that would end UNMIK, despite strong support for doing so among the original intervening parties.[20]

Kosovo's Emergent Autonomy

In the aftermath of Kosovo's 2008 declaration of independence, the international community began to incorporate local elites selectively into leadership roles in the slowly developing institutions dedicated to Kosovo's national defense. Unfortunately, these measures were not nearly as egalitarian or inclusive as those proposed earlier by the ISSR. Florian Qehaja, executive director and cofounder of the Kosovar Center for Security Studies, points out the emergence in state institutions of what

---

[19] See Marc Weller, *Contested Statehood: Kosovo's Struggle for Independence* (Oxford, UK: Oxford University Press, 2009), 123–25. Russia's late opposition to these plans came after a troika made up of representatives from its government, as well as from the European Union and the United States, engaged in a series of negotiations lasting three months. In the ad hoc intergovernmental body's report to the UN Secretary General, the governments jointly argued that "the parties were unable to reach an agreement on Kosovo's status," stating that "neither side was willing to yield on the basic question of sovereignty." See *Report of the European Union/United States/Russian Federation Troika on Kosovo*, S/2007/723 (New York. UN Security Council, 2007). As a result, Secretary General Ban Ki-moon reiterated the position sustained in the letter sent from his office on 26 March 2007. It stated to the president of the Security Council that "having taken into account the developments in the process designed to determine Kosovo's future status, I fully support both the recommendation made by my Special Envoy in his report on Kosovo's future status and the Comprehensive Proposal for the Kosovo Status Settlement." The International Court of Justice noted in its advisory opinion on Kosovo's independence that it was Russia's opposition amid these developments that led the drafters of the Security Council Resolution in pursuance of the Ahtisaari Plan—France, Italy, the United States, Belgium, and the United Kingdom—to withdraw the measure from consideration. See "Accordance with International Law of the Unilateral Declaration of Independence with Respect to Kosovo, Advisory Opinion," International Court of Justice, 22 July 2010.

[20] Henry H. Perritt Jr., *The Road to Independence for Kosovo: A Chronicle of the Ahtisaari Plan* (New York: Cambridge University Press, 2010), 42–45.

he refers to as a *KLA elite*. This term captures the prominent political position assumed by former commanders in the KLA, and the willingness of the international community to recognize their authority for the sake of ensuring stability. These individuals, who identified overwhelmingly as Albanian Sunni Muslims, brought with them a deep fear of the reemergence of conflict, as well as an abiding motive to prepare for the return of hostilities. Their experience of fighting a war from a position of disadvantage—in terms of numbers, armaments, and know-how—made them permanently wary of renewed fighting.[21] The rise of the KLA elite coincided with the greater authority accorded to the state over the security sector. Once ratified, the country's new constitution required that "the Republic of Kosovo has authority over law enforcement, security, justice, public safety, intelligence, civil emergency response, and border control within its territory."[22]

Despite this legal transformation that entailed greater local control over the security sector, the international community remains deeply invested in its role of oversight and management regarding Kosovo's security. The Ahtisaari Plan serves as a reference for the development of institutions that protect and defend Kosovo, with the International Civilian Office (ICO) now acting as a watchdog for deviations from the terms of the settlement. The ICO regularly intercedes in the security sector when its staff receives reports of inconsistencies between the laws and policies of the Kosovar government and the stated goals and expectations of the Ahtisaari Plan. The European Union's (EU) "rule of law mission"—known as EULEX—similarly intervenes on a regular basis in matters of internal policy making. NATO's Kosovo Force (KFOR), which initially conducted the full panoply of necessary peacekeeping operations,

---

[21] Qehaja, *International or Local Ownership?*, 61–42.

[22] Republic of Kosovo Const., art. CXXV.

serves as another example of consistency rather than change amid the country's transition to formal independence. Its mandate has never been substantially altered in writing since the force's initial creation. Despite more than 80 percent reduction in boots on the ground—from 50,000 troops at the height of KFOR's presence in 1999, down to 8,000 after independence in 2008—NATO remains a constant arbiter of key security questions. KFOR's operational emphasis has shifted toward maintaining peace in the northern part of Kosovo, especially around Serbian enclaves. Some progress toward greater autonomy has occurred: KFOR has transferred most border control duties, which it previously entirely controlled, to the KPS.

With regard to the development of Kosovo's early strategic culture, nowhere has the push and pull of international versus domestic influences been more consequential than in the creation of the Kosovo Security Force (KSF). This institution was designated to supersede the vestiges of the KLA and the formally disbanded KPC. After the conclusion of the UN special envoy on Kosovo status's work, Ahtisaari and his staff prescribed the establishment of the KSF in precise terms. Ahtisaari recommended 2,500 active, lightly armed personnel, with 800 servicemembers in reserve. Their remit would be limited strictly to disaster relief and civil protection. This idealized role for the KSF was connected to the international community's demands for demilitarization and disbandment with dignity, which sought to eliminate militant, nationalist organizations that aimed to ensure Kosovo's security.[23] Embedded in this approach was a deep and abiding belief that these kinds of informal institutions would damage Kosovo's position as an avowedly multiethnic society, with a security sector that equally represented all minority communities.

---

[23] Ade Clewlow, *The Kosovo Protection Corps: A Critical Study of Its De-activation as a Transition* (Oslo: Norwegian Institute of International Affairs, 2010).

The steps to disband existing militias and discourage new ones stirred resentments. First, these maneuvers operated on the presumption that Kosovo's Albanian population, which understandably felt under threat, should not maintain militias to protect their communities. In addition, the KSF's strictures created a backlash because they compromised the careers of many fighters who saw themselves remaining involved in national defense. The KSF would not allow more than 50 percent of the KPC to become part of the KSF. Uncertainties associated with the reintegration of KPC members became an important concern. Civilian employment for the majority of the KPC members was tied directly to the preservation of international support for Kosovo's statehood. This progression of events seemed overbearing to vocal representatives of Albanian communities. The experience left a lasting mark on relations between them and international staffs focused on Kosovo's security sector. The decision to dissolve an existing institution—the KPC, which had a locally defined role to provide national defense—and to supplant it with a new organization with an internally defined role led to a great deal of concern among local elites about how Kosovo would address future security threats.

Dependence and Self-Determination

The Kosovar government's dependence on external support remains tied to the influence of international organizations that were present during the nascent stages of security institution development. Despite steps toward autonomy and the advent of independence in 2008, Kosovo's government still relies heavily on the international community. This reality limits its capacity to resist external decisions and recommendations, even in cases where local politicians express concern that overreliance on outside assurances might not fully ensure Kosovo's stability and security.

Kosovo's dependence on external actors stems primarily from the legacy of international support for its economy. This fundamental aspect of life in the country—which affects the livelihood and long-term prospects of every man, woman, and child—is at the forefront of decision making. Desperate to improve Kosovo's position as the third poorest country in Europe, local politicians will do whatever is necessary to avoid creating worse economic circumstances. This necessitates shrewd thinking that preserves existing productivity and streams of income, which are tied to programs supported through aid initiatives. Although Kosovo's GDP per capita (U.S. dollars) has increased from $1,088 in 2000 to $3,641 in 2016, economic dissatisfaction and related civil unrest remain high.

There are three major components comprising Kosovo's economy. First, there is the unusually small sector of local industry that constitutes 16 percent of GDP: 10 percent is in manufacturing and 11 percent in agriculture. Ninety-seven percent of enterprises in Kosovo are most appropriately termed *microenterprises*, with 1–9 employees in total.[24] Second, remittances from the diaspora bolster the economy, but this stream of proceeds is hard to measure and subject to considerable change from year to year. Many members of the diaspora invest in property in Kosovo or undertake short-term, profit-bearing projects.

Finally, there is the flow of aid. The World Bank estimates a steady decline from approximately U.S. $782 million in 2000, down to the present $370 million in 2016.[25] Because Kosovo's 2017 GDP totals only $6.6 billion, even the current reduced flow of aid accounts for a significant proportion of economic activity. Nearly 18 percent of GDP originates from

---

[24] *Republic of Kosovo Systematic Country Diagnostic* (Washington, DC: World Bank, 2017), 35.

[25] "Net Official Development Assistance and Official Aid Received, Kosovo," World Bank, updated February 2018.

international aid agencies tied to governments. When considered in conjunction with Kosovo's significant unemployment rate, 32.7 percent, and its particularly worrisome youth unemployment rate, 57.6 percent, the importance of sustaining aid to maintain societal stability becomes apparent. Kosovo has remained one the world's highest per capita recipients of aid for nearly two decades.[26] The initial emphasis of donors on helping refugees has moved toward enhancing competitiveness and building enterprises. Nonetheless, habits have emerged among policy makers to incorporate the distribution of aid into many political calculations. Even comparatively small reductions in aid would make certain enterprises unsustainable and have ripple effects across communities. These alterations can produce significant negative effects and adverse political ramifications for those in power.

It should come as no surprise that, in this context of deep economic dependence, a tendency toward acquiescence to international actors arose and came to pervade Kosovo's early strategic culture. The most obvious manifestation of this phenomenon appeared in the stilted and slow transition of stated aims in Kosovo's *National Security Strategy* (NSS) documents. In a democratic country, comprehensive policy statements typically seek to set out the strategic framework that will guide the security sector. Such documents tend to propose a vision of reform that scrutinizes existing strengths to secure citizens and the state from threats on the horizon.[27] Kosovo's NSS was prescribed by the final negotiations on its status, which included the provision that "Kosovo shall develop a security strate-

---

[26] *Republic of Kosovo Systematic Country Diagnostic*, 55–57.
[27] See definition derived in *Democratic Control of Armed Forces*, *National Security Policy* (Geneva, Switzerland: Geneva Centre for Democratic Control of Armed Forces, 2005).

gy."[28] The constitution later created the prerogative for local political actors to produce this document, providing explicitly that "the Security Council of the Republic of Kosovo in cooperation with the President of the Republic of Kosovo and the Government develops the security strategy for the Republic of Kosovo."[29] The parliament's 2008 Law on the Establishment of the Kosovo Security Council (KSC) suggested that this agency would undertake the drafting and publication of the document, which was planned to be initiated in 2009.[30]

Despite the legal basis for a robust local role in the creation of the NSS, international influence proved overwhelming. Due to a lack of capacity in the KSC, Kosovo's Ministry of Internal Affairs took on the task of coordinating the production of the first strategy document. The ministry organized several working groups, focused on legal questions, technical concerns, and measuring risks, as well as a few dedicated to specific threats. Two civil society representatives were recruited to be members. Only one international expert contracted with the ministry to serve as a consultant and was tasked with assessing the next logical steps to mature the NSS. Although this open and pluralistic process promised to emphasize local perspectives on security affairs, involvement by the ICO in Pristina quickly altered the course of policy formulation. Drawing on its mandate to ensure compliance with the Ahtisaari Plan, staff from the ICO monitored the meetings of the ministry's working group members. Rather than simply invoking its executive powers, the ICO undertook a remarkable intervention.

This endeavor entailed putting forward a framework for the NSS that melded international best practices with steps

---

[28] *Comprehensive Proposal for the Kosovo Status Settlement* (Vienna, Austria: Office of the Special Envoy of the Secretary General for the Future Status Process for Kosovo, 2007), 49.
[29] Republic of Kosovo Const., art. CXXVII.
[30] Law on the Establishment of the Kosovo Security Council, Law No. 03/L-050.

toward European integration. Officers from the ICO sought to establish a document that did not address certain areas of concern for Kosovo's ministerial staffs. The areas of concern not addressed were the pursuit of full international recognition, the rise of violent extremist movements, the position of communities in northern Kosovo, wide-ranging quarrels with Serbia about territorial demarcations, the fate of minority groups, and many other disputes. These topics were omitted with the justification that directly addressing them would potentially worsen threats and trigger inflammatory reactions. Kosovo's international partners urged a focus on less controversial policies.

The ICO recommended vague references to human security, without ever fully defining the term. International experts associated with the organization proposed assessing risks and threats through indicators related to economic, environmental, and societal hazards, which avoided any pronouncements regarding military and political insecurity.[31] As a result, capable members of the technical working group in charge of the drafting process resigned. Once critical members of this team removed themselves from the process, the ICO proceeded to radically change the draft, producing a document that was fundamentally different from the original version's outlines.[32] The ICO's approach was based on a deep concern that hostilities must be avoided at all costs. Nonetheless, the impact of this initial experience created a lasting impression that the management of the Kosovo security sector would remain deeply influenced by the international community.

The ICO's input was based on a preference for noncon-

---

[31] The 2009 NSS ended up loosely following the division of threats put forward by political scientists Buzan and Weaver in their delineation of national security concerns among democratic states. See Barry Buzan et al., *Security: A New Framework for Analysis* (Boulder, CO: Lynne Rienner, 1997).

[32] Dennis Blease and Florian Qehaja, "The Conundrum of Local Ownership in Developing a Security Sector: The Case of Kosovo," *New Balkan Politics*, no. 14 (2013): 1–20.

frontation as well as a belief that such an approach would contribute to broader stability in the Balkans. To this end, the original NSS presumed that the Balkans were becoming a peaceful and democratic neighborhood, and that Kosovo was a multiethnic society committed to cosmopolitan values. For example, the NSS proposed that Kosovo profess a foreign policy in line with the European Union's creed, "United in Diversity." Unfortunately, this idealistic approach was not mirrored by adjacent states that, unlike Kosovo, did not include international actors in the formulation of their security policy. A comprehensive Serbian security strategy was published in 2009, which stated that "the introduction of the so-called KSF represents a serious threat toward the existing regime of arms control and . . . is detrimental toward the balance of powers in the region."[33] These developments were not lost on local government officials in Kosovo, who believe that Kosovo has no choice but to take antagonistic neighbors seriously.

A delayed reaction among Kosovar security elites in 2012 eventually produced an entirely separate process that resulted in the preparation of the *Strategic Security Sector Review* (SSSR). The SSSR was primarily shaped by local bureaucrats and politicians and intentionally sidestepped any past or future disagreements with the NSS. The specific aim of the government was to enact a legal framework for the transformation of the KSF. The work leading to the SSSR began with a wide-ranging review of the security sector and involved input from diverse ministries and agencies across Kosovo's national government. The document addressed many issues, including the specter of Islamist extremism. The document proposed retaining the KSF and creating the Kosovo Armed Forces (KAF) to be dedicated to addressing external threats. After the publication of the

---

[33] *National Security Strategy of the Republic of Serbia* (Belgrade: Government of Serbia, Ministry of Defence, 2009), 8.

SSSR in March 2014, the prime minister of Kosovo, Hashim Thaçi, announced that the KAF would be comprised of 5,000 active members and 3,000 reserve members, with the establishment of a Defense Ministry to follow by 2019.[34]

Polling conducted among Kosovo's population by the Pristina-based Centre for Security Studies demonstrated wide support for this approach. A survey conducted within one year of the change in policy suggested that 87 percent of citizens in both domestic and rural contexts preferred the decision to transform the KSF into the KAF. The option to maintain the KSF as it was implemented by the NSS was supported by only 6 percent of respondents.[35] These statistics indicate the divergence between local perspectives on strategic matters and the desire of international partners to promote change in that collective outlook. The maturation of the policy making process and the similar growth of an organic strategic culture was in step with the sentiments of Kosovo's citizens.

It is crucial to note that these dynamics are not endemic to Kosovo. "Getting to Denmark," as Francis Fukuyama said regarding state-building, is harder than many international organizations assume it to be. The creation of stable, democratic societies has proven elusive in many post-conflict and so-called failed states. Recipes for effective institutions, a homegrown and credible postwar defensive posture, and local preferences for formal rules over informal relationships are hard to come by. As Fukuyama suggests, a general theory of development aimed at supplying these attributes of the state, based on stu-

---

[34] The following report was issued to flesh out the prime minister's proclamation: *Analysis of Strategic Security Sector Review of the Republic of Kosovo* (Pristina: Government of Kosovo, 2014).

[35] Qehaja, *International or Local Ownership?*, 93–94. For important context, see Nihat Çelik's work indicating this disposition for outward-looking defense forces throughout the Balkans. Nihat Çelik, "The Evolution of Civil-Military Relations and Democratization in the Balkans," *Journal of Regional Security* 7, no. 1 (2012): 1–15.

dious attempts to replicate the historical progress of successful peers, will likely remain a chimera for the foreseeable future.[36] Yet, less than perfect outcomes do not dissuade bodies such as the ICO from attempting to shape the security policies that salve consciences more than solve problems posed by hostile environments.

A Domestic Crucible: Specialist Chambers and War Crimes

Veterans of the bureaucratic processes associated with the creation of national security documents might read the previous section with wise skepticism. Official tracts like the NSS and SSSR often obscure as much as they reveal, reflecting the tendency of political actors to put forward pretexts to mask their true interests and motives. Just as with any writing associated with public affairs, these valuable pieces of evidence deserve special scrutiny and should be considered in tandem with other evidence. For that reason, it is important to examine an issue that reveals less savory—and perhaps less flattering and presentable —aspects of Kosovo's relationship with its surrounding region and the wider world. The prosecution of Kosovar war criminals provides just such a cross section of fears, concerns, and tensions, which occasionally spill into public view.

Before addressing this touchstone issue, it is important to explain the turmoil that often engulfs controversial legislation in Kosovo. Unsurprisingly, it does not take much to stir the fears of the voting public who are still traumatized by war. The country's internal deliberations exhibit turbulence that is common among states attempting to transition to democracy after suffering decades of authoritarian rule. This disputatious political environment usually creates turmoil when sensitive issues

---

[36] Francis Fukuyama, *State-Building: Governance and World Order in the 21st Century* (Ithaca, NY: Cornell University Press, 2004), 29.

are raised such as the fate of Serbian ethnic enclaves and unresolved border demarcations. Compromise on these issues can easily be portrayed as jeopardizing the territorial integrity for which blood was shed. Sentiments fueled by recent memories easily change into destructive behavior.

The most familiar trope associated with media coverage of Kosovo arose from the opposition's repeated use of tear gas in the parliament chamber to stop votes on pending legislation. These episodes should not be read as blanket evidence that Kosovo's government perpetually slips into disarray. For one thing, these dramatic acts are essentially the protestations of political minorities in a given debate who believe they have no other recourse short of violent confrontation with the majority. They indicate a desperation to maintain the status quo. It would be wrong to ignore the seriousness of these incidents, or to claim they do not represent deep dysfunction in Kosovo's domestic political system. However, they provide very little substance or insight for those studying Kosovo's strategic culture. Discerning relevant insights from the froth and wailing that accompanies legislation on war crimes prosecutions requires careful attention.

The Kosovo Specialist Chambers, which seek to prosecute war criminals, have had an irreversible impact on Kosovo's strategic culture. Focused on the period from 1998 to 2000, the Specialist Chambers were created to deal with the findings first put forward by Dick Marty, a Swiss politician. Authored under the auspices of the Council of Europe, his report argued that war crimes had been committed by the Albanian paramilitary organizations that fought to free Kosovo from Serbia.[37] The Specialist Chambers, which function as a court, were commissioned by the state specifically to address alleged crimes com-

---

[37] Dick Marty, *Inhuman Treatment of People and Illicit Trafficking in Human Organs in Kosovo* (Strasbourg, France: Parliamentary Assembly of the Council of Europe, 2010).

mitted by soldiers and leaders in the KLA. These individuals are accused of committing atrocities against "ethnic minorities and political opponents" during and directly after the war of liberation.[38] Early on in Kosovo's development as a state, these revelations led EULEX to prompt its Special Investigative Taskforce to examine the council's claims further. EULEX prosecutors ruled that facts were adequate for the prosecution of war crimes and crimes against humanity. Although EULEX initiated prosecutions of the approximately 1,200 war crimes cases referred to it by UNMIK, 500 were dismissed and 600 remain pending within various offices of prosecutors. EULEX has initiated 51 new cases; yet, since independence, it has only fully adjudicated 15 war crimes cases.[39]

Because of the perceived slow-moving and limited prosecution of these cases by existing bodies such as EULEX, the international community has consistently pushed for further measures. The Specialist Chambers is an institution dedicated to this purpose. Years of advocacy in this regard led the Kosovo Assembly to enact a series of laws, culminating in a constitutional amendment in 2015, to allow accused Kosovar citizens to be tried outside the country in The Hague. Created by Kosovar law, the court's location ensures adequate protection for witnesses.[40]

Progress toward achieving the stated goals of the Specialist Chambers has stalled. Wave after wave of opposition to the commencement of adjudication are to blame. Most recently, in late 2017 and in early 2018, legislation was introduced in Kosovo's parliament to prevent the court from beginning its proceedings. These measures were supported by Kosovo's rul-

---

[38] "Kosovo Court to be Established in The Hague," Government of the Netherlands, 15 January 2016.

[39] Bernd Borchardt, "EULEX and War Crimes," EULEX Kosovo, 14 March 2017.

[40] Marija Ristic, "New Kosovo Court Confronts Witness Protection Fears," *Balkan Insight*, 3 October 2016.

ing coalition—the Democratic Party of Kosovo, the Alliance for the Future of Kosovo, and the Initiative for Kosovo. For now, this scheme has failed to pass. Despite its legal preservation, the Specialist Chambers recently lost its chief prosecutor, David Schwendiman, who resigned in March 2018.[41]

Two crucial security-related themes are revealed by these bottlenecks, which demonstrate aspects of Kosovo's incipient strategic culture. First, popular and political sentiments are firmly set against the legal processes to prosecute crimes undertaken by militias against the Serbian military, as well as unrelated acts committed under the banner of that cause. Interestingly, most of the crimes on the docket for prosecution have been reported by Kosovar citizens against their fellow citizens. Individual members of the national community feel wronged by political killings, acts of sexual violence, and many other nefarious activities. Yet, the Specialist Chambers serve as a potential threat to nationalist sentiment, which is a vital constituent component of Kosovo's strategic culture.

The war of liberation remains a sacrosanct narrative that emphasizes the moral righteousness of freedom fighters seeking independence. As such, it must not be challenged, even if the aggrieved parties are fellow ethnic Albanians. Those who dispute this view are to be shunned. Countrywide polling on public confidence in the chambers' witness protection policies reflect these biases. Individuals who might betray the publicly accepted account of the war do not believe they will escape retribution for doing so, regardless of the setting (in domestic courts, or abroad in the Netherlands—at the chambers' proposed location). Others believe that testimony, which complicates the Manichean narrative to be an unforgivable offense in itself. For example, 82 percent of ethnic Serbs and nearly one-

---

[41] Marija Ristic, "Kosovo Special War Court Prosecutor to Step Down," *Balkan Insight*, 15 February 2018.

half of all ethnic Albanians do not believe it is safe for witnesses to deliver testimony. Nonetheless, strong majorities of both Albanians (64.8 percent) and Serbs (53.2 percent) feel war crimes committed from 1998 to 2000 must be adjudicated.[42] The contradictions embedded in this public opinion reflect the crosscurrents in collective beliefs about Kosovo's position in the region. For the country to remain secure, it is believed, the moral claims that justified its fight for independence must remain untarnished. These imperatives still undergird its right to exist.

Second, the controversy surrounding the Specialist Chambers reflects the sense of persecution and embattlement shared among ethnic Albanians. Despite widespread public campaigns to educate the public about the domestic, legal basis for the court, opposition to it remains associated with the plight of Albanians in a region previously dominated by Serbia. Parliamentary attempts to close the Specialist Chambers emanated from movements among the public that articulated this view. A petition filed by KLA veterans became the clearest expression of the belief that the court served an inherently discriminatory purpose. They and others in Kosovo's society argued that, because the Specialist Chambers will indict only Kosovo citizens, it will not fairly address crimes committed by Serbian forces. These claims, of course, disregard the fact that the court was created by the Kosovo state specifically to prosecute crimes of citizens under the jurisdiction of the state. Nevertheless, the continued pull of these arguments shows no signs of abating. Polling from last year indicated that, among ethnic Albanians, 76.4 percent view the court's mandate as unacceptable because it emphasizes war crimes and crimes against humanity mainly associated with the KLA. Fifty-one percent of the same group

---

[42] Michael James Warren et al., *Public Perception of the Kosovo Specialist Court: Risks and Opportunities* (Utrecht, Netherlands: PAX, 2017), 4–6.

are willing to protest further if KLA fighters are eventually indicted, and 36 percent are willing to take action—beyond protesting—to stop the prosecution of KLA members.[43] Here again, a sense of embattlement, persecution, and the necessity of preserving the capacity for defense are reflected in popular opinion.

Conclusion

This chapter has evaluated Kosovo's strategic culture, providing insights not ordinarily available in the vast literature on the country's position as a post-conflict society. The capacious definition of strategic culture set out by this volume undoubtedly may be mapped onto the information presented here. Elites in Kosovo most certainly have developed identifiable shared beliefs, assumptions, and patterns of behavior, constructing for themselves ways, means, and ends for achieving security.

When assessing these attributes, it is clear in Kosovo's case that they have just as often been shaped through interactions with supportive external actors, as through encounters with hostile, nearby foes. A central theme of this analysis has been to highlight the agency of a people whose destiny has been so fully determined, since independence, by outside actors— NATO, the UN, the EU, and others. Simply because these non-Kosovar actors have influenced Kosovar strategy does not mean that Kosovars have themselves failed to muster responses based on their own conceptions of strategy. Throughout the period of Kosovo's earlier development, local elites have accepted, rejected, and modified the standards and concepts provided to them by outsiders. In fact, the response by local political elites—to the dissolution of the KPC, to the NSS, and to the Specialist Chambers—indicates their development of methods

---

[43] Warren et al., *Public Perception of the Kosovo Specialist Court*, 1–6.

for coping with and altering aspects of their strategic policy that they do not fully control. As a result, their interaction with the international community has often showcased the independent will of the Kosovar people. To deny this would be to disregard their agency altogether.

Another important theme, which naturally complements this primary finding, relates to the divergence of Kosovar and international perspectives on what its security policy should be. Members of the international community overseeing Kosovo's transition have often put forward ambitious plans. They seek to change Kosovo through a regime of good governance, replete with administrative steps that celebrate Kosovo's multiethnic status and that avoid direct confrontation with problematic neighbors. This path—according to well-meaning, international actors—is the way to maintaining peace and prepare the country for European integration. Kosovars on the ground often view the time line and horizon of threats differently. They argue pragmatically for policies that will address existing threats from countries around Kosovo that could seek to dominate it. Obviously, these conflicting visions are the result of different strategic cultures. Local politicians, bureaucrats, and members of the media often advocate for traditional means of wielding hard power while formulating national security priorities and policies that comport with short-term goals. The conflict between this vision and that of external actors remains highly consequential.

Unlike other cases evaluated in this book, Kosovo has not developed strategic culture by deriving it directly from an uninterrupted, long history of wars conducted as an independent state. However, it would be wrong to suggest that this amounts to evidence that Kosovars themselves have yet to understand their role in a dangerous neighborhood of states. In a world that has turned against the kind of Western intervention that brought Kosovo into being, this autonomy will remain crucial. Kosovars will likely need to seize the reigns of their policy prerogatives, act on their assessment of local challenges, and prepare for the turbulence resulting from further American and European disengagement.

CONCLUSION

by Matthew R. Slater, PhD

Parting Thoughts on the Strategic Culture Approach

The methodological issues associated with data from different levels of analysis are increasingly gaining the attention of practitioners and academics. Strategic culture falls into this category by existing between the seams of the international, domestic, and individual levels of analysis.[1] Strategic culture's controversy is amplified by existing at the crossroads of academic disciplines, including international relations, history, geography, and sociology. The evidence of strategic culture's value may be found in the fact that, despite its disruptive nature, it has endured and even flourished since Jack L. Snyder brought attention to the term in 1977. There are advantages and disadvantages to existing in the theoretical middle ground: strategic culture offers researchers additional choices to consider, but it is also more vulnerable to criticism since it defies traditional methodologies. This concluding chapter will provide an overview of research insights that emerged from the five case studies. These findings are reviewed below in thematic sections.

---

[1] Strategic culture is primarily focused at the domestic level of analysis but also considers strategic leadership (individual) and the impact of regional and international influences.

Which History?

The application of strategic culture requires the author to use history in its proper context. However, that is often easier said than done. Which history of the state is the most relevant? The overreliance on recent history could miss the subtle influences from hundreds of years ago, or what may be referred to as a reductive fallacy that tries to reduce complexity and in the process changes or distorts facts.[2] An author who wants to prove the persistence of certain cultural patterns of behavior from the distant past may be biased toward finding reoccurring behavior in modern governments. The case studies from this book provide a few suggestions on how to effectively assess the past in combination with current state dynamics.

In the Brazilian case study, Denise Slater points out that the recent accommodation between the military and the Brazilian Ministry of Foreign Affairs, or Itamaraty, was key to melding the nation's strategic culture into a coherent whole. A common view between the two institutions began to coalesce after the last regime change, when the military gave way to democracy in 1985. Since that time, the two organizations worked together, and despite their differences forged a shared view of Brazilian national interests and how to achieve them.

The China case study relies primarily on Confucianism to explain the elements of consistency in its strategic culture, but through the lens of Marxist-Leninist ideology. Christopher D. Yung points out how difficult it is to isolate the individual aspects of a strategic culture with thousands of years of history. How does one begin to evaluate which era is most relevant to the collective whole? The advent of the most recent political system is an important starting point, but Yung also assesses the traditions, philosophies, and influences of the past

---

[2] David Hackett Fischer, *Historians' Fallacies: Toward a Logic of Historical Thought* (New York: Harper and Row, 1970), 172.

against current political dynamics. The Chinese revolution had a sweeping impact on traditional political, economic, and social systems, but Confucianism continues to influence Chinese decision making.

The Brazilian case suggests that strategic culture analysis should begin with recent history—perhaps with the most recent regime change. The China example tells us about the importance of understanding recent regime changes along with the deeply embedded traditions of the past.

New States, Old States, and Strategic Culture

Strategic culture assessment is dependent on historical trends and patterns that form the foundation for a historical narrative. Because of this, one might assume that understanding the strategic culture of a state with an established history is less complicated than the study of the emerging history of newly founded states. The logic of this argument is that the longer the history, the greater the likelihood of discerning consistent patterns of behavior.

However, there are also disadvantages to researching states with an extensive history. The Afghanistan and Chinese case studies show us that the researcher must possess expertise that extends potentially hundreds of years into the past to adequately assess strategic culture. Not only must the author understand the breadth of a state's history, but they must also be able to assess what parts of history endure to impact current strategic culture. Choosing which history to focus on is likely the most controversial aspect of the strategic culture concept: an overreliance on a particular era may bias the results of a study. More recent states such as Kosovo, with its newly forming institutions, allow for less complexity about what to assess, although the cultures within the state may have celebrated histories that must be factored into strategic culture assessment.

What is meant by the term *new states*? The most fundamental meaning insinuates that the government of a state was recently established. A new political regime will undoubtedly impact strategic culture due to changes in bureaucracies, laws, foreign policy, a reordering of interest groups, and many other revisions. However, governmental change should not assume a completely different path for the historical narrative. Subgroups of the state may possess histories that are much older than the political order, as in the case of Kosovo and the Albanian and Serbian subgroups. This begs the question: At what point in time should a researcher begin their historical assessment? For example, the current Brazilian government began in 1985, it became a republic in 1889, and declared its independence from Portugal in 1822. Many Brazilians believe the state's inception occurred after defeating the Dutch in 1654. Which of these dates should be used as a starting point to evaluate Brazil's strategic culture?

The most accurate answer is that every case study will be unique. One method suggested by the Chinese and Brazilian case studies is to approach strategic culture from the perspective of recent history and then move back through time, carefully eliminating the historical outliers from your assessment. If the author chooses to ignore a seemingly influential era in a state's history, they must do so with caution and justify why there is a lack of relevance. This method assumes that the most recent political, military, and social institutions will likely have the most importance to current strategic culture.

The Kosovo case study demonstrates that, although history will always be a major component of strategic culture assessment, the lack of state history does not preclude the value of strategic culture assessment. Studying the emerging institutions, politics (internal and external), and group dynamics in Kosovo demonstrates the cognitive dissonance that will shape the character of its emerging strategic culture. The lack of consistency in strategic decision making made George Bogden's assessment more challenging. He highlighted the domestic-level sources of influence and their clash with regional and international institutions. The author was able to provide a coherent picture of Kosovo's strategic range of options, despite the new state's emerging policies and institutions.

Dealing with Composite Regimes

Failing states frequently capture the interest of U.S. foreign and defense policy makers. They are often the epicenter of regional instability because they foster competition among neighboring states; produce refugees, causing both internal and external displacement; attract outside and internal terrorist groups; and disrupt regional trade. Failing states usually possess fragmented governance. The central government typically maintains a strong presence in the capital and in other urban centers or nearby provinces. Competing political or ethnic groups may control spaces ranging from an entire province to more localized areas such as a village.

This patchwork of governance, or composite regimes, challenges the utility of strategic culture.[3] Is strategic culture only useful in the case of states with developed internal strategic communities? Vern Liebl's Afghanistan case study demonstrated that regardless of the limitations posed by composite regimes, the search for unifying history and institutions within Afghanistan yielded interesting results. Despite the limited control of the federal government, there were integrating features such as Pashtunwali and manteqa that help explain Afghanistan's consistently decentralized historical narrative. The mutual disdain and resistance against invaders permeate all ethnic groups, and despite the political autonomy from each other and the federal

---

[3] The term *composite regimes* was coined by Charles Tilly and Sidney Tarrow. It is defined as: "Regimes in which different systems of rule shape the contentious repertoires of different populations." Charles Tilly and Sidney Tarrow, *Contentious Politics* (New York: Oxford University Press, 2007), 163.

government, they historically come together under manteqa to resist outside attack. These informal but universal features of Afghanistan's strategic culture inform practitioners about unifying characteristics that begin at the micro level and impact behavior at the national level. The Afghanistan case study may be a starting point for researchers dealing with the challenges of applying strategic culture to highly decentralized states. Rather than focusing on federal-level institutions or policies, perhaps more answers will be found at the lower levels of governance.

National Strategic Communities

Chapter two mentions the term *national strategic communities*. This refers to the institutions, groups, or individuals that are internal to the state and make a significant contribution to the strategic culture. The Chinese case study refers to the Communist Party as the primary national strategic community, whereas the Brazilian case study refers to the military and the Brazilian foreign service as integral institutions. The Kosovo case study focuses on the office of the prime minister, the KLA, and outside influences such as the International Court of Justice, among others. The Afghan strategic community is decentralized among multiple competing power centers, but the common thread between them is the Pashtunwali and the manteqa. These examples show that the concept of national security communities is flexible and allows a great deal of latitude for the researcher. This flexibility may be viewed as a disadvantage if one's purpose was to construct theory, but works to the advantage of a practitioner who seeks to describe the unique strategic culture of a given state.

There is a great deal of potential research by employing the perspective of national strategic communities. Understanding the composition of national strategic communities is an important first step. How should the components of national strategic communities be categorized? What is the relationship between them? Other lines of inquiry may compare the national strategic communities of individual states to determine if types of strategic communities will generate similar state behavior. Modeling tools such as social network analysis may help decipher how state strategic communities are organized and how decisions are made that lead to a standardization of national strategic community types. Although similarities between communities would likely be superficial and still require research to understand the unique elements of individual states, a taxonomy may facilitate comparative analysis and further the study of strategic culture.

The Challenge of Dependent States

The case studies in this book highlight the challenges of applying strategic culture to small, newly formed states, such as Kosovo. Small states may be heavily influenced by external actors due to their relative vulnerability. The influence of the European Union on Kosovo's domestic politics demonstrates this point. When applying strategic culture to dependent states, it is important to discern the level of outside influence. Is it possible to separate an independent strategic culture in these cases and how does that influence the research? What is the dividing line between independent decision making and choices heavily shaped by the outside power? The European Union seems intent on developing Kosovo to be multicultural even when the majority Albanian population deeply distrusts the minority Serbian ethnic group.

Even in these cases, strategic culture assessment provides relevant descriptions of state behavior by explaining the source of outside influences, their agenda, and how they interact with the domestic strategic community to achieve their ends. Not only does this explain current policy choices for the dependent state, but it may also help qualify how the struggle between the domestic strategic community and outside influences generates patterns of behavior.

Research Suggestions and Follow-on Research

Particular lines of research could augment the current strategic culture body of literature, including the topics of complex strategic cultures, weak states, the role of subgroups, strategic narratives, the concept of national strategic communities, and the effect of transnational actors and diasporas.

Complex strategic cultures offer a unique challenge to researchers.[4] When studying complex strategic cultures, the author should be prepared to refute counterarguments within the literature because of the unsettled nature of the state in question. Having issued a "proceed with caution" statement, the exploration of these kinds of cultures may also be the most rewarding because fewer studies tend to exist. If the author presents a well-documented, cogent assessment, it increases the likelihood of broad acceptance in the community of practice.

When studying strategic cultures, the researcher should intentionally include subgroups or informal institutions—even in cases where a strong central government is present. Subgroups may play a role in shaping the strategic culture that might be missed if not specifically targeted in each study. In the case of failing states, the need to include subgroups is self-evident due to a lack of central government control. Even in states with strong central governments, researchers may strengthen their case by including prominent subgroups and institutions. In the final assessment they may not be specifically

---

[4] The use of the term *complex* refers to strategic cultures lacking historical precedent, possessing political decentralization, or may simply be under researched so the composition of their strategic culture remains partially understood.

addressed as a key influence but their impact at the outset of study may help the researcher frame their line of inquiry.

More research would help shed light on the role of the strategic narrative in shaping strategic culture and how to apply it within the context of strategic culture. A strategic narrative may be defined as "representations of a sequence of events and identities, a communicative tool through which political actors —usually elites—attempt to give determined meaning to past, present, and future in order to achieve political objectives."[5] A deeper understanding of a state's strategic narrative is important for several reasons. By identifying a strategic narrative, such as Christopher D. Yung and Denise Slater in the China and Brazilian case studies, the author may be able to conclude the interests, methods, and goals of state governments.

The case studies indicate that the convergence of a national strategic community, usually triggered by external events, plays a formative role in strategic culture. In the case of Afghanistan, an enduring pattern reemerges when an invasion evokes a common response from major subgroups. The perceived threat to the Amazon forced a coherency to Brazilian strategic culture that had not been present during the prior 20 years. China uses the traditional fear of foreign intervention combined with the unity provided by the Communist Party to fuel its national cohesion. Kosovo's strategic culture seems to be defined by its perpetual fear of Serbian aggression. Researchers may want to begin their assessment by understanding how a state perceives current threats, and how that may or may not act as a catalyst to unite a state's strategic community toward a common purpose.

The role of transnational actors and diasporas are other topics of interest not covered in the case studies but suggested

[5] Alister Miskimmon et al., *Strategic Narratives: Communication Power and the New World Order* (New York: Routledge, 2013), 5.

as part of a standard strategic cultural framework by Blagovest Tashev in chapter 1. In many states, as demonstrated by the European Union's influence in Kosovo, transnational actors may exert influence on a state's decision-making process and outcomes. Diasporas may act as a hidden force of influence in some states such as Lebanon. There are now at least twice as many Lebanese living abroad than the state's current population of 6 million. The diaspora may be important actors in the economies and politics of some states and their influence should be considered.

GLOSSARY AND ABBREVIATIONS

Arab League	Regional multinational organization of Arabic-speaking countries in Africa and Asia
ASEA	Association of Southeast Asian States
BLA	Baloch Liberation Army
CENSIPAM	Center for the Management and Operation of the Amazon Protection System (Centro Gestor e Operacional do Sistema de Proteção da Amazônia)
Durand Line	The 2,640-kilometer (1,640-mile) border between Afghanistan and Pakistan created by an agreement between Sir Mortimer Durand, secretary of the British Indian government, and Abdur Rahman Khan, the emir of Afghanistan. It has served as the official border between the two nations for more than 100 years
EIC	East India Company
Embrapa	Brazilian Agricultural Research Corporation (Empresa Brasileira de Pesquisa Agropecuária)
ESCEME	Brazilian Army's Command and Staff College (Escola de Comando do Estado-Maior do Exército)
ESG	Brazilian Army's War School (Escola Superior de Guerra)
EU	European Union
FARC	Revolutionary Armed Forces of Colombia (Fuerzas Armadas Revolucionarias de Colombia)
Group of Seven	Also known as the G7. The Group of Seven, or G7, is an international economic organization consisting of the seven largest International Monetary Fund-described advanced economies in the world:

215

	Canada, France, Germany, Italy, Japan, the United Kingdom, and the United States
ICO	International Civilian Office, a watchdog for deviations from the terms of the Ahtisaari Plan settlement in Kosovo
INPA	National Institute for Amazonian Research (Instituto Nacional de Pesquisas da Amazônia)
INPE	Brazilian National Institute for Space Research (Instituto Nacional de Pesquisas Espaciais)
Irredentism	The policy of the incorporation or reincorporation of territory historically or ethnically related to one political unit but under the control of another
ISAF	International Security Assistance Force
IS-KP	Islamic State-Khorasan Province
ISSR	*Internal Security Sector Review* (ISSR) initiated by the UN in Kosovo. This program monitored the operation of security institutions, proposing means of increasing their capacities and producing greater self-sufficiency
Itamaraty	The metonym for the Brazilian Ministry of Foreign Affairs (Ministério das Relações Exteriores)
jirgas	Manteqa committees, part of an informal governance system based on the Pashtunwali
KAF	Kosovo Armed Forces
KFOR	NATO's Kosovo Force
KGB	Komitet Gosudarstvennoy Bezopasnosti or "Committee for State Security"
KLA	Kosovo Liberation Army
KPC	Kosovo Protection Corps
KPS	Kosovo Police Service
KSC	Kosovo Security Council
Kosovo Specialist Chambers	Charged with prosecuting war crimes
manteqa	Composed of several villages and is the actual social and territorial unit of rural Afghanistan
MINUSTAH	United Nations Stabilization Mission in Haiti (Mission des Nations Unies pour la Stabilisation en Haïti)

NATO	North Atlantic Treaty Organization
OAS	Organization of American States
PIN	Brazilian National Integration Plan (Plano de Integração Nacional)
PLA	People's Liberation Army, the armed forces of China
RADAM	Radar Mapping Project (Radar da Amazônia), an initiative pioneered by the Brazilian government to map the country's natural resources in the Amazon using radar and imaging sensors
Rational actor model	Assumes that decision makers are rational and would choose actions that help them achieve their goals
Realism	The study of the material characteristics of the environment to understand the behavior of states
PRODES	Satellite Monitoring of the Brazilian Amazon Forest (Programa de Monitoramento da Floresta Amazônica Brasileira por Satélite), which is the Brazilian government's satellite program to monitor deforestation in the Amazon
PS/ACTO	Permanent Secretariat/Amazon Cooperation Treaty Organization
Schengen Agreement	The treaty that led to the establishment of the Schengen Area in Europe, in which internal border checks have been abolished
SDF	Japanese Self-Defense Force—military after World War II
SISFRON	Integrated Border Monitoring System (Sistema Integrado de Monitoramento de Fronteiras)
SIVAM	Amazon Surveillance System (Sistema de Vigilância da Amazônia)
SRGC	The special representative of the secretary general, an individual tasked by the UN with coordinating all aspects of the civilian and military organizations acting to secure Kosovo
THAAD	A U.S. missile defense system known as Terminal High Altitude Area Defense
UN	United Nations
UNESCO	United Nations Educational, Scientific, and Cultural Organization

Universal harmony	A Chinese notion of harmony based on shared values as opposed to Western ideals of balance
UNMIK	United Nations Mission in Kosovo
USSR	Union of Soviet Socialist Republics
VOC	Verenigde Oost-Indische Compagnie, or the Dutch East Indies Company
Warsaw Pact	A mutual defense organization that put the Soviets in command of the armed forces of the member states. Signed in Warsaw, Poland, the treaty included the USSR, Albania, Poland, Romania, Hungary, East Germany, Czechoslovakia, and Bulgaria

INDEX